compiled by

JEAN NYBURG

BACHMAN & TURNER

Yours Tastefully
Jean Nyburg

First published, 1984

ISBN : 0 85974 126 5

Text illustrations by Jean Nyburg
Front cover design by Eric Souster
Section frontispieces by Kenneth Baxendale

A BACHMAN & TURNER BOOK

Published by Bachman & Turner
Maidstone Industrial Centre, St Peter Street
Maidstone, Kent ME16 0ST.
Typesetting by Triste Ltd., Shirley, Croydon.
Printed and bound in England by
K.L. Litho Ltd., London EC2A 4HU.

HOW IT ALL BEGAN . . .

One day I went to a Cancer Relief Committee meeting — only the second I had ever attended.

Jean Nyburg

The usual subject—dear to every Committee's heart came up—'We must make some money! How about producing a Cookery Book?'

"What a good idea," they all said. Then I suddenly realised they were looking at me.

"You'll do it, won't you? You've been a caterer all your life."

"But," I protested, "I don't know anything about producing books."

"Nonsense — you're a librarian now (part time — 6 hours a week!) So you can do it."

"I'll try," I said weakly. So I went away and thought and thought . . .

It was supposed to be the recipes of everyone in the village, and was to be advertised initially in the local "Chagford Bulletin". They would all write in with their recipes, and that would be that.

But then I began to dream of extending the appeal on a national scale.

So I wrote to Prince Charles because we live in his Duchy. I thought he might take an interest, and he did . . . by return of post.

Similarly, our Patron, Her Royal Highness, the Duchess of Kent graciously sent a recipe at once.

Then it started to get out of hand . . .

Flushed with success, I wrote letter after letter to MPs, stage and TV stars, sportsmen, Church dignitaries, photographers, climbers, musicians and so on.

The busier the person, from Mrs Thatcher onward, the more prompt was the reply. His Holiness the Pope was unable to provide a recipe but he gave his blessing for the success of this book.

Then there was a publisher to find. This was a trying time, but eventually that was sorted out, with a lot of help from my friends who found me a publisher.

Expenses were kept to a minimum — just postage and paper and a few telephone calls.

To cover these, I was lucky enough to have several small cheques and quite a number of gifts of food and books for sale or to raffle, from Kenco, Danish Bacon, Cheeses of Switzerland, McDougalls and Duff & Trotter, and several private donations.

So now all our profits and royalities can go to our Funds. There are no staff to pay, no overheads, it is all done for love.

Thank you to all the people who contributed and gave me advice, and most of all, thanks to my dear husband.

He is a wonderful cook — and has tried out many of the recipes himself. Between us, we have wrecked our figures for ever, trying out all the "Oh! Dear" recipes — and many others, too, but it has all been worth it.

The recipes are printed as they were received — so if there are any mistakes, please forgive me.

Thank you for buying the book,
and helping Cancer Relief.

Jean Nyburg,
Chagford, Devon
1984

A MESSAGE FROM:
THE NATIONAL SOCIETY FOR CANCER RELIEF
HELPING PEOPLE WITH CANCER — NOW

One in four people in the UK will suffer from cancer at some time during their lives.

We all know families who have been affected by this cruel disease. Some patients are cured but many, who continue to suffer, face difficult practical problems and need skilled medical care and support for themselves and their families.

The National Society for Cancer Relief, founded in 1911 by Douglas Macmillan, provides patients with very positive practical help. This help is given through the Society's Macmillan fund in the following four ways.

In-patient care

Cancer Relief builds Macmillan homes where doctors and nurses, skilled in the most modern methods of pain and symptom control, give individual care to patients who cannot benefit from treatment aimed at cure.

The dedicated staff aim to create a relaxed atmosphere where patients can feel at home and relatives are welcomed and encouraged to participate in the nursing care. Great importance is attached to giving strong emotional support both to the patients and their families.

To date, the Society has funded the building of 12 Macmillan homes and given them to the National Health Service to run. Cancer Relief has also part-funded six other homes which are run by independent charities.

Home care nursing

Most cancer patients would prefer to be looked after at home, surrounded by their relatives and friends. Cancer Relief's Macmillan home care nursing services help to make this possible.

Macmillan nurses work with GPs and community nurses, and they visit patients on a regular basis.

They are specially trained to advise on pain control and to give emotional support and comfort to the whole family.

With this extra help patients can remain at home for much longer.

Cancer Relief finances Macmillan nurses for their first three years of service. After that they are taken over by the Health Service or a local charity.

At present, there are just over 200 Macmillan nurses throughout the country. Double that number is needed to provide an acceptable level of home care nationally.

continued

Patient grants

Caring for a cancer patient at home can create serious financial problems for a family. A previously self-sufficient member suddenly becomes totally dependent and often the husband or wife has to stay at home to nurse the patient.

Bills accumulate and hardship is frequently the outcome. Cancer Relief moves in swiftly to help. Macmillan grants are given to thousands of patients and their families bringing real relief from money problems and restoring the family's sense of independence.

Education for doctors and nurses

Special skills in cancer care, particularly pain control, have been developed quite recently, and many medical and nursing staff have not yet gained the necessary expertise because of the lack of training opportunities.

To help solve this problem Cancer Relief is creating new education centres and financing special training courses for medical and nursing students. As a result, these new and special skills are now being used in more general hospitals where, inevitably, most cancer patients are cared for.

For further information on Cancer Relief's work contact:
The National Society for Cancer Relief, Room B, Michael Sobell House, 30 Dorset Square, London NW1 6QL   Telephone: 01-402 8125

With grateful acknowledgements to

HRH Prince Charles,

His Grace The Archbishop of Canterbury

and

HRH The Duchess of Kent,

who is the Patron of

the National Society for Cancer Relief,

as well as to the many others

who have contributed

to making this book possible.

CONTRIBUTORS

CONTENTS

continued

MEAT

VEGETABLES and VEGETARIAN

PICKLED!

continued

NEARLY SLIMMING SNACKS

EVER SO SLIGHTLY FATTENING

OH! DEAR! (Sweets & Puddings)

*   *   *

continued

Soups, Pâtés and other Temptations

"CAUGHT on the HOP" SOUP

A ring at the bell, and there are two of your oldest friends on the doorstep. They haven't come for lunch — just passing through on their way to Cornwall.

You were just going to finish off that ½ tomato and the end of the cheese for your lunch —

Give them a drink and dash into the kitchen. There, lurking in the fridge are 2 cold potatoes, that tomato and some gravy from yesterday's dinner.

Put it all in the liquidiser with an onion or two, a clove of garlic and that tiny bit of cabbage, and switch on.

Pour into a pan, season, heat gently for 15 minutes, or as long as it takes to drink your sherry/gin/orange juice — grate cheese on top. *A triumph in minutes!*

Jean Nyburg,
Chagford

16

CAULIFLOWER SOUP

Main course soup
Serves 4

1 large cauliflower
1½ pints chicken stock
¼ tsp salt
2 oz butter
6 tbs flour
10 fl oz milk
½ tsp pepper or chervil
¼ tsp mace
1 egg yolk
2 tbs single cream
½ tsp lemon juice

1. Make a roux. Add stock and milk and simmer 2–3 minutes
2. Add chopped cauliflower. Keep a few florets for decoration
3. Add pepper, and simmer ½ covered for 15 minutes
4. Mash cauliflower and return to pan
5. Beat egg yolk and cream together
6. Beat in hot purée a little at a time until 8 tbs have been added
7. Pour mixture into pan, beating all the while
8. Cook for 2–3 minutes — still stirring — and add extra florets at the last minute.
   DO NOT LET SOUP BOIL OR IT WILL CURDLE
9. Stir in lemon juice and test seasoning
   VERY FILLING!

Kathleen Jeken,
Leeds

GAZPACHO

A delicious cold soup

2 ripe tomatoes peeled and seeded
1 large cucumber peeled and seeded
½ red or green pepper seeded
½ Spanish onion
4 green onions
2 cloves garlic
½ tsp salt
¼ tsp pepper
½ cup dry crumbs
3 tbs olive oil
2 tsp white vinegar
½ cup cold water
½ lb ice cubes
1 cup cold water

1. Finely chop tomato, cucumber, pepper and onions. Place in a large bowl
2. Grind garlic, salt and pepper and bread crumbs with a pestle and mortar
3. Add to mixture in bowl
4. Slowly add oil and vinegar, stirring well
5. Pour in ½ cup water; stir well
6. In a 2 cup measure put 1 cup water and enough ice cubes to make up to a 2 cup level
7. Pour this into the gazpacho bowl and chill in a cool place. Before serving, remove any bits of ice
8. Decorate with finely chopped cucumber, onion, tomato, slices of hard boiled egg and plain croutons. Serve with French bread.

John Dankworth C.B.E. A.R.C.M.
Famous Jazz Musician

18

GREEN LENTIL SOUP   Czech recipe

1 lb. Canadian green lentils
Handful of dried mixed vegetables
Small bunch chopped parsley
1 soup spoon plain flour
2tbs oil
2 beef stock cubes
1 lb soaked prunes
1 soup spoon sugar
2tbs lemon juice
Salt and pepper
Dutch smoked sausage

1. Soak lentils overnight. Drain and throw away water
2. Put lentils in pan with a little salt and pepper, the dried vegetables and parsley. Add 4 teacups water to each teacup of lentils
3. Cook 25—30 minutes
4. Make a roux with flour and oil, and thin with some of the soup
5. Add to rest of soup in pan and stir in
6. Crush beef cubes into soup and stir
7. Add soaked prunes and bring to the boil
8. Cook gently for 2—3 minutes
9. Add sugar and lemon juice and taste for flavour
10. Add chunks of skinned Dutch smoked sausage at the last minute.

Mrs David Astor,
St John's Wood, London

KIWI and STRAWBERRY SOUP

An exotic cold soup for a SUMMER DINNER PARTY

This recipe was given to me by Louis Segal, the proprietor of Frederick's Restaurant in Camden Passage, London, and was specially created by his head chef, Jean-Louis Pollet, for this book.

1 large peeled potato
1 large peeled onion
1 leek (only the white part)
1½ pts chicken stock
¼ pt double cream
20 gr butter
2 Kiwis — diced
1 punnet of strawberries
Few leaves of mint

1. Dice potato and onion and gently fry in the melted butter the onion and leek and then the potato without colouration
2. Add chicken stock and simmer slowly for 20 mins with seasoning
3. Remove from gas and let soup cool
4. When cold, add cream and the strawberries and blend until the ingredients have been properly puréed
5. Serve cold with diced Kiwis, and garnished with mint leaves.

Louis Segal,
Frederick's Restaurant,
Camden Passage, London

20

LEEK SOUP

1 lb leeks, thinly sliced
1 oz butter
1 pint liquid (½ milk, ½ water)
1 oz porage oats
1 bay leaf
Salt and black pepper

1. Lightly fry leeks in butter until the rings are clear (about 3 minutes)
2. Stir in porage oats and add liquid
3. Bring to the boil, add seasoning and bay leaf
4. Reduce to simmering point, and simmer for about 5 minutes at most.

   EAT — there will be none for tomorrow

Penny Lees,
Sticklepath, Devon

21

LONDON PARTICULAR!!

A good PEA SOUP for a cold winter's day

3½ pints stock
1 carrot
12 oz split peas
2 onions
1 stick celery
1 clove garlic
4 rashers streaky bacon

1. Add peas to stock
2. Cook for ½ hour
3. Sweat onions, carrot, celery, garlic and bacon for 10 minutes
4. Add peas and stock. Cook for 40 minutes, or until peas are soft and mushy
5. Sieve or liquidise
    Decorate with croutons, chopped parsley and a swirl of cream.

TIP *Grow some early peas in a tray in the greenhouse. When the tips are about 2 ins high, cut like cress and use to give flavour to the pea soup.*

Jean Nyburg

LUDLOW BROTH

Serves 6

A good winter soup, based on a regional recipe

2 oz butter
2 lamb chops
2 chopped onions
2 sticks celery
2 diced carrots
2 oz pearl barley
2 tbs Worcester sauce
1 tsp walnut ketchup
3 pints beef stock
Salt & pepper
Chopped chives — basil — parsley
4 oz shredded cabbage

1. Melt butter in a large pan and fry chops until well browned on both sides
2. Add all other ingredients except herbs and cabbage
3. Bring to the boil and simmer for 1½ hours — or ½ an hour in the pressure cooker
4. Strain liquid from chops. Take meat from bone. Return to pan with liquid. Add herbs and cabbage
5. Simmer gently for 5 minutes
6. Adjust seasoning and serve with crusty bread.

Dilys Evans,
Ludlow

ORANGE SOUP

A summer soup

¼ pint soured cream
1 onion
11b tomatoes
1 carrot
Lemon rind
¾ pint stock
Juice of 2 oranges
1 orange rind
Bay leaf
1½ oz butter
6 peppercorns
1 tsp sugar
¾ tbs flour

1. Sweat onion and carrot. Add rind
2. Squeeze oranges and add juice to pan
3. Add tomatoes, stock, peppercorns and sugar
4. When boiling, lower heat and cook for ½ hour
5. Liquidise
6. Add soured cream

Su Bowater,
Chagford

PARSNIP and ONION SOUP

2 parsnips
1 onion
3 oz butter
1 clove garlic
1 tbs flour
1 tsp curry powder
2 pints hot beef stock
Salt and pepper
¼ pint cream

1. Peel and slice parsnips and onion
2. Melt butter in large heavy pan
3. Add sliced parsnips and onion and crushed garlic
4. Mix well to coat vegetables with butter
5. Put lid on pan and cook over a low heat for
   10 minutes, shaking pan now and then
6. Sprinkle over flour and curry powder and mix well
7. Blend in hot stock. Simmer for 20 minutes
8. Liquidise
9. Just before serving — add cream.

Sir Peter Mills,
MP for West Devon

25

SPICY TOMATO SOUP

½ oz butter
1 onion
½ oz flour
Blade of mace
1 lb tomatoes
4–6 peppercorns
1 clove of garlic
salt to taste
1 tsp paprika
Bouquet garni
1¼ pints chicken stock
½ oz sago
Glass of port or red wine

1. Sweat onions in butter
2. Add everything except alcohol
3. Cook for 30 minutes
4. Add port or red wine
5. (Pour out a glass for yourself!)
6. Serve soup with brown bread croutons and sprinkle with chopped chives.

TO BE REALLY "HAUTE"
ADD A SWIRL OF CREAM

Jean Nyburg

TOMATO and APPLE SOUP

1½lbs ripe tomatoes
1½ pints stock
1 medium onion, chopped
1 medium cooking apple — chopped and peeled
¼ tsp dried mixed herbs
½ clove garlic, crushed (optional)
1 tbs tomato purée

1. Quarter tomatoes
2. Heat 1 tbs oil in large frying pan
   Add tomatoes, onion and apple
3. Cook on low heat with the lid on for approx
   15 minutes or until vegetables are soft. Transfer
   to large saucepan
4. Add stock and tomato purée, herbs and garlic.
   Bring to the boil
5. Simmer for 30 minutes
6. Rub through a sieve. Season to taste
7. If soup is not thick enough, thicken with a little
   cornflour
   Serve with croutons and Parmesan cheese.

Neil Smith F.L.C.M.
World Famous Classical Guitarist
Bolton, Lancs

VEGETARIAN SOUP

A main course soup

½ lb beans
½ lb pearl barley
4 oz margarine
4 pints stock
Bouquet garni
Seasoning

1. Put chopped onion in pan with margarine and sweat gently for 5 minutes
2. Add 2 pints of vegetable stock
3. Add bouquet garni, then the barley and beans
4. Cook for 2 hours
5. Add up to 2 pints more stock
   Serve with chunks of hot wholemeal bread

Anne Angas,
York

CHICKEN LIVER PÂTÉ

Quick and easy

Takes about 10 minutes to make.
A great standby for cocktail canapés,
appetisers for dinner parties or just a
lunchtime snack with Melba toast.

1 large onion — sliced
Pinch of basil
2 cloves garlic — crushed
Pinch of thyme
½ lb chicken livers
Salt and pepper
½ lb Krona margarine or butter

1. Sweat onions and garlic in butter or margarine —
   Do not brown
2. Prepare chicken livers and cut up
3. Add chicken livers and herbs to pan
4. Cook for a few minutes
5. Put everything in the liquidiser
6. Season to taste
7. Transfer to crock. Cover with butter or margarine
8. Chill.

DO NOT FREEZE because the texture changes and
becomes gravelly!

Jean Nyburg

ECONOMICAL PÂTÉ

½ lb sliced pig's liver
1 small onion
½1b sausagemeat
1 clove garlic
4 rashers streaky bacon
1 egg
1 round tsp parsley
1 level tsp salt
½ level tsp mixed herbs
Ground black pepper

1. Mince liver, onion and garlic
2. Add sausagemeat and beaten egg
3. Add herbs and seasoning and cover with foil
4. Bake at 380°F for 1½ hours in a 11b bread tin, placed in a container of water

If quantities are doubled, cook for 2 hours or more.

Josephine Binney R.I.B.A.
Sherborne, Dorset

EGG and MUSHROOM PÂTÉ

4 hard-boiled eggs
2 tbs margarine
2 tbs whipped cream
2 tbs lemon juice
1 clove garlic
1 tbs chopped parsley
6 oz sliced, sautéed mushrooms
Few drops of tabasco
Lemon slices
Lettuce leaves
Sprig of parsley

1. Liquidise eggs with cream and 1 tbs of lemon juice
2. Whip clove of garlic round mixing bowl and mix eggs in it
3. Toss mushrooms in lemon juice and add to eggs. Season
4. Add chopped parsley and tabasco
5. Spoon into bowl and chill—or pile on lettuce leaves
6. Garnish with lemon twists and parsley and serve with Melba toast.

EGG & PEPPER PÂTÉ

As above, but substitute 1 large green pepper for the mushrooms.

Jean Nyburg

PIG'S LIVER PÂTÉ

Another well tried and easy recipe

1 lb pig's liver
1 lb butter
2 onions
Bay leaf
1 clove garlic — crushed (optional)
Salt and pepper to taste

1. Cook liver for 20 minutes at Gas Mark 5 (375°F)
2. Mince cooked liver with raw onion and garlic
3. Beat in butter
4. Season
5. Place in greased casserole and top with bay leaf
6. Leave to set.

Jean Nyburg

SARDINE PÂTÉ

Serves 4

4½ oz can of sardines in oil
Small pkt Philadelphia cheese
1 tsp lemon juice
1 dsp chopped chives
Salt and pepper
Dust of paprika
Lemon slices
Parsley to garnish

1. Drain oil from sardines
2. Mash sardines with cheese, lemon juice and chives
3. Put into a crock, dust with a little paprika and chill
4. Garnish with lemon slices and parsley
5. Serve with Melba toast.

THIS PÂTÉ WILL FREEZE VERY WELL

Neville and Mary Ward R.I.B.A.
London
"Ward Associates"
Architectural Design Partnership

SMOKED OYSTER PÂTÉ

In commercial photography, clients often drop in unexpectedly or stay on after a shoot and it is useful to be able to offer them something more interesting with their drinks rather than the usual nuts or crisps.

2 tins smoked oysters
3 level tsps gelatine
1 carton sour cream
1/3rd cup mayonnaise
1 bunch spring onions, chopped
Salt and pepper

Dissolve the gelatine according to the packet instructions.

Combine all ingredients with either fork or food processor.

CHILL and SERVE

Robin Adler F.R.S.A.

AVOCADO MOUSSE

Very easy

2 avocados
1 tsp Worcester sauce
1 tsp grated onion
½ pint double cream
2 eggs, separated
1 pkt gelatine
½ cup home-made mayonnaise

1. Mash avocados
2. Add sauce, onion, cream, egg yolks and mayonnaise
3. Dissolve gelatine
4. When partially set, fold in whipped egg whites
5. Pour into wetted 1–1½ pint mould
6. Chill.

Present on crisp lettuce hearts
and serve with Melba toast

Jean Nyburg

CRAB MOUSSE

Cornish

1 tin crab soup
¼ pint double cream
¼ pint peeled prawns
1 tbs mayonnaise
1 stiffly beaten egg white
1 envelope gelatine
Salt and pepper
Mace and garlic
Cucumber and chives

1. Mix soup, cream and mayonnaise in blender
2. Fold in egg white
3. Dissolve gelatine in water and mix in, after seasoning to taste
4. Set. Decorate with chives and prawns
5. Serve with iced cucumber salad.

**Perry Tregaskis,
Truro**

SMOKED SALMON MOUSSE

6 oz smoked salmon trimmings
¼ pint mayonnaise
3 tbs water
½ oz gelatine
¼ pint double cream
Juice of ½ lemon
Salt and pepper
Pinch of cayenne
2 drops tabasco
3 egg whites
Finely chopped parsley

1. Blend or process smoked salmon and mayonnaise for just long enough to finely chop the salmon
2. Combine gelatine with water and stir over low heat until melted
3. Add gelatine mixture to salmon and mayonnaise with lemon juice. Season with salt, pepper, cayenne and tabasco. Blend for a few seconds to mix
4. Turn into a bowl and chill in the refrigerator until mixture begins to set
5. Whip egg whites until stiff
6. Whip the cream until thick
7. Fold the cream and then the egg whites lightly into the mousse base
   Turn into rinsed mould or individual ramekins and chill in refrigerator at least 2 hours
8. Sprinkle over parsley just before serving. Serve with hot toast or French bread and butter.

Mary Rankin,
Gidleigh, Devon

STILTON MOUSSE

6 oz Stilton
2 oz Cheddar
½ pint single cream
2 egg whites
1 oz almond nibs
½ oz gelatine
2 egg yolks
Seasoning

1. Grate Stilton and Cheddar together
2. Dissolve gelatine
3. Whisk egg whites
4. Add egg yolks to cheese
5. Pour gelatine down side of bowl. Fold or cut in egg whites
6. Sprinkle almonds on top.

Anne Nevill,
London
Y.T.S. Training Officer
in Catering

BAKED EGGS with SHRIMPS

Serves 4

1 small tin shrimps or prawns (or 4 oz frozen)
4 eggs
1 tsp chopped parsley
1 oz grated cheese
¼ pint béchamel sauce
½ oz butter
Cayenne pepper
Salt to taste

1. Boil eggs for ten minutes and plunge into cold water
2. Peel and chop thoroughly
3. Make béchamel sauce
4. Add chopped eggs, parsley and shrimps
5. Season and add butter
6. Spoon into individual fireproof dishes and sprinkle with grated cheese
7. Brown in hot oven or under grill and serve at once.

Robert Runcie,
The Archbishop of Canterbury

GAZPACHO MOULD

Serves 4—6

A deliciously easy start to a dinner party — because it can be prepared the day before.

1 pkt lemon or lime jelly
¼ tsp salt
1 cup boiling water
¾ cup cold water
1 tbs vinegar
2 tbs lemon juice
1 tbs grated onion
1½ cups diced vegetables, composed of equal parts cucumber, green pepper, avocado and tomato — (vary according to taste)

1. Combine gelatine and boiling water
2. Stir until dissolved
3. Add vinegar, lemon juice, onion, salt and cold water
4. Chill until thickened
5. Fold in diced vegetables
6. Pour into mould
7. Chill until firm.

Sue Price,
Chagford, Devon

GRAPEFRUIT APPETISER

Something different!

1. Cut out the centre of a large decapitated grapefruit
2. Mix the fruit and juice with a generous amount of cottage cheese
3. Line the grapefruit case with cut up pieces of lettuce
4. Fill with mixed grapefruit and cheese.

EXCELLENT "STARTER"

Dame Ninette de Valois D.B.E.

JANSSON'S TEMPTATION

Swedish

6 medium raw potatoes
3 large onions
12 anchovy fillets (Norwegian or Swedish)
Salt and pepper
1 tbs toasted breadcrumbs
2 tbs butter
1 – 1½ cups cream and milk
3tbs brine from anchovy can

1. Peel and slice into thin strips the 6 potatoes
2. Slice onions and sauté in the butter,
   then spread on bottom of a buttered baking dish
3. Cover onions with anchovy fillets, then layer of
   potato, seasoning and top with breadcrumbs
4. Bake in a hot oven 425° F for 15 minutes
5. Pour over the cream, milk and brine and bake for
   a further 20 minutes until potatoes are soft.

Sheelagh Knox,
Throwleigh; Devon

42

MARINATED MACKEREL

Swedish

For each 1 lb of fish: —
2—3 tbs sugar
2—3 tbs salt
Fresh dill or dill WEED **not** *seed*
Coarsely ground black pepper

1. Clean and fillet mackerel
2. Rub sugar well into both sides of fillets
3. Rub salt in also
4. Cover bottom of shallow dish with chopped dill
5. Lay fillets skin down
6. Sprinkle with pepper and dill
7. Put remaining fillets head to tail on top —
   SKIN SIDE UP
8. Cover with dill and let fish marinate in fridge for at least 48 hours.
   CUT LIKE SMOKED SALMON TO SERVE

A delicious hors d'oeuvre which needs no cooking, is prepared in advance and will keep for a week in the fridge.

SAUCE:

2 tbs wine vinegar   1 tbs sugar
Sunflower oil   chopped dill
4 tbs mustard (can be Dijon)

1. Mix vinegar, sugar and mustard
2. Slowly add oil, stirring all the time, as if making mayonnaise until consistency is that of thin mayonnaise
3. Stir in chopped dill. *GREAT!*

Daphne Jackson,
Chagford, Devon

A SIMPLE WAY with PRAWNS

Prawns
1 tbs butter
Pepper
Salt

1. Peel fresh prawns and place in a bowl
2. Melt butter in saucepan, taking care not to burn
3. Add pepper and salt and pour the mixture on the cold prawns

The resulting flavour will prove a delightful surprise for those who have not tried it before.

Robin Ray
Music buff, famous for
"Face the Music"
and many other shows

TCHININ

A fish flavoured hors d'oeuvre

7 oz tin of sardines
5 hard boiled eggs
2 tbs mayonnaise
1 tbs lemon juice
1 tsp Worcester sauce
2 tbs whipped cream
Salt, pepper, chives
Nuts, lettuce hearts

1. Drain oil from sardines and remove all the bones
2. Chop eggs
3. Liquidise all ingredients except the cream
4. Adjust the seasoning and add cream
5. Put mixture in a forcing bag and decorate the lettuce hearts
6. Dust with paprika and sprinkle with chopped nuts and chives.

Jean Nyburg

HOW TO USE LEFT OVER BREAD

To make seasoned breadcrumbs:-

add *½ tsp marjoram*
¾ tsp basil
½ tsp garlic salt
¼ tsp onion powder
¼ tsp ground black pepper
½ cup parmesan

1. Lay bread on a baking sheet and dry thoroughly in a cool oven
2. Crush or liquidise bread and stir in other ingredients
3. Store in an airtight tin in a cool place.

Fish

ARTHUR'S FISH PIE

2 lb smoked haddock
Some prawns or shrimps
4 tomatoes
4 hard boiled eggs
Breadcrumbs
Ingredients for cheese sauce

1. Boil fish for about 8 minutes, and flake into a greased pie dish
2. Add chopped up eggs and prawns
3. Make a fairly strong cheese sauce
4. Pour into the dish and mix well
5. Cover with breadcrumbs and then with the sliced tomatoes
6. Dot with butter
7. Cook in a medium oven for about 30 minutes, and then brown under the grill.

"YUM! YUM! YUM!
I am drooling at the mere thought!"

Arthur Marshall,
"Call my Bluff"
BBC TV

BUTTERY KEDGEREE

A typical breakfast dish from Victorian days.
Nowadays a good lunch or late supper dish.

1½ lbs thick smoked haddock fillets
3 oz butter
1 chopped onion
Up to 8 fl oz level in measuring jug of
  long grain rice
16 fl oz boiling haddock water
¾ tsp curry powder (Madras)
3 hard boiled eggs
1 tbs lemon juice
3 heaped tbs parsley, freshly chopped
Salt and freshly ground black pepper

1. Put haddock in pan and cover with 1 pt water
2. Bring to boil, put on lid, simmer for 8 minutes
3. Drain water into measuring jug
   Put fish on dish, cover with foil and keep it warm
4. Melt 2 oz butter and sweat onion in it for 5 minutes
   Stir in curry powder, cook for ½ minute, then stir
   in measured rice and add 16 fl oz haddock water
5. Stir. When it gets to simmering point, put on lid
   and cook gently for 15 minutes until rice is tender
6 Remove skin from fish, flake fish. When rice is
   cooked fork in flaked fish, eggs, parsley, lemon juice
   and 1 oz butter
7 Cover with tea towel and heat gently for 5 minutes
   Season and serve.

Richard Briers,
famous for "The Good Life"
and many other shows

FISH BREAKFAST

Place fairly large pieces of cooked and skinned fillets of kippers or any kind of smoked fish, in a fireproof dish, with mustard, pepper and cayenne pepper.

Cover with coarsely chopped hard boiled egg.

Cover again with cream and
a knob of butter.

Put in the oven at 350° F
until brown.

Clementia Raikes,
Linwood, Hants

FISH FORK SUPPER

1 lb white fish (cod)
4 oz prawns
1 lb smoked fresh fish (haddock)
4 oz chopped mushrooms
Bay leaf
6 hard boiled eggs
1 oz melted butter
6 oz grated Cheddar cheese
Milk
5 fl oz double cream
Peppercorns
Bran flakes to cover
Parsley to decorate
Mace
A little fish stock

1. Poach fish gently in milk with slice of onion, bay leaf, mace (2 pieces) and 6 white peppercorns
2. Flake when cold and add chopped eggs, prawns, melted butter, mushrooms and fish stock to moisten
3. Put all the above in a buttered flan dish and add cream
4. Sprinkle grated cheese over top and cover with bran flakes and a little butter
5. Bake at 350° F for 35—40 minutes
6. Decorate with parsley before serving.

Mrs Sheila Engelse,
New Malden, Surrey

GRAVLAX

"A recipe from ICELAND where I presided over a TV festival and nearly died and went to heaven eating SALMON . . ."

This recipe is for an 18lb SALMON
 BUT
It can be scaled down to whatever kind of piece you buy
 AND EVEN
made with MACKEREL at the fag-end of the housekeeping!

This is the original	**Mustard sauce for Gravlax**
18 lbs salmon	*½ cup cooking oil*
16 tbs salt	*2 tbs French vinegar*
½ tsp saltpetre	*1 tbs Swedish sweet*
16 tbs sugar	*mustard or Dijon*
30 whole peppercorns	*1 tbs sugar*
(ground)	*1 tbs honey*
5 tbs fresh or dry dill	*DILL to personal taste*
	STIR. Serve in a sauce boat on the side.

1. Have fishmonger bone the salmon
2. Mix all spices and rub into filleted salmon
   Put fillets together, skin side out
   Place on tray or dish, rubbing rest of spices into the skin
3. Keep in cool place (or fridge) for at least 48 hours, turning occasionally
4. Pour away liquid that forms. Slice the fish into palm sized pieces ¼inch thick (not long bits like smoked salmon)
   Serve with bread or toast and butter and mustard sauce.

**Sian Phillips,
well-known Stage and TV star**

London

GREY MULLET with bacon & sage

Serves 4

2 grey mullet — something over 1 lb each
4 good rashers of **smoked** *back bacon*
8 sage leaves
4 oz dry vermouth
2 oz breadcrumbs
2 oz thick fresh cream
2—3 oz butter
Salt and pepper

1. Scale and clean fish and slash in 4 or 5 places on each side
2. Chop bacon and sage leaves finely together (use moulinette if possible)
3. Put some of the resulting paste onto the cuts on the mullet
4. Mix breadcrumbs with remaining paste
5. Season well and stuff in cavities of fish
6. Butter a baking dish liberally
7. Put fish in dish and bake at 400°F or Gas Mark 6 for 15 minutes
8. Pour over vermouth and continue to bake till done, about 10—15 minutes
9. Pour cream on to fish and give a further 2 minutes
10. Serve immediately and *HOT,* on *HOT* PLATES!

**Sir Michael Hordern,
National Theatre**

53

KIPPERS

"My favourite dish
is
LOCH FYNE
Kippers
Grilled on both sides
until very
crisp."

Baron Sieff of Brimpton,
London

MACKEREL, HOW TO SMOKE
in a biscuit tin

Preparing the mackerel

With a sharp knife, cut a fillet from each side of mackerel, wash fillet and dry using kitchen paper.

Take an empty biscuit tin, place inside a small grill; one from your grill pan will do.

Sprinkle 2 dessertspoons of sawdust over the bottom of the tin. Lay the fish fillet on the grill.

Sprinkle with salt.

Put the lid on the tin and place on the stove — preferably outside.

After about one minute, smoke will come out under the lid.

In another 2—3 minutes, turn off the heat and leave to cool with the lid still on.

The lid is left on 10—15 minutes, depending on the flavour you like best.

Sawdust is obtainable from fishing tackle shops.

Ted Tuckerman,
Fishing expert on TSW-TV

MRS PENNINGTON'S FISH PIE

"This is the best recipe for FISH PIE that I know; very simple, and taught me at my mother's knee. It's her own invention".

Use any combination of fish — haddock, cod, prawns, but be sure 50% is smoked — very flavoursome.

Allow ½lb fish per person maximum

Poach fish from frozen 7—8 minutes
Skin and flake

Hard boil some eggs — 1 per person
Chop them up

Make a fairly thick cheese sauce in the usual way, with mustard and nutmeg included

Combine all the above in a buttered baking dish

Mash potatoes for the topping
Top these with golden breadcrumbs, paprika and sliced tomatoes

Heat through in the oven (on a baking sheet as it may overflow).

Michael Pennington
National Theatre

"MY" FISH DISH

Fillets of plaice or whatever
1 banana
Oil or butter
¼lb mushrooms
Anything else that takes your fancy or happens
to be lying around

1. Lay fish in shallow dish
2. Surround with sliced banana, mushrooms etc
3. Sprinkle with salt, pepper and oil or butter
4. Cover with foil and cook for 10 minutes at
   Gas Mark 5
   Remove foil and cook for 5 more minutes
5. If you are feeling extravagant, add some cream
   before serving.

Yvonne St Claire Anderson,
Chagford, Devon

PETER BULL'S KEDGEREE

"Everyone (well nearly everyone) has their method of making this delicious dish, but I think mine is the best (natch)."

Get quite a lot of smoked haddock (or cod, if the former is not available/too expensive)
Boil it for a bit
A packet of rice must then be boiled until ready (not flabby and stuck together)
Having carefully searched for bones which may still be lurking in the fish, meld the rice and haddock together
Add a few drops of Worcester sauce,
1 tsp curry powder and ½ packet parsley
Squeeze some fresh lemon on the whole thing
Personally, I add a tin of tuna fish and a tin of prawns with their brine.

As regards the obligatory hard boiled eggs I serve them after the guests have helped themselves or been helped by A.N. Other to the main dish.

The secret success of this operation lies in liberal mixing with butter to keep the concoction moist, whilst stirring over the stove.

One of the great advantages of making Kedgeree is that it tastes even better the 2nd day or even the 3rd. A 4th might be hazardous, and jolly good luck to one and all!

continued on next page

PETER BULL'S KEDGEREE continued

A final word of advice.

You can't be too careful about the bones.

I was once a guest on an American TV show, demonstrating this dish, and in the final segment was supposed to be seen tasting the dish (it is almost unknown in the States) with my glamorous hostess.

I saw to my horror that there was a huge bone sticking from the fork she was raising to her mouth.

I managed to halt her in mid-air, so to speak, but I doubt if many Americans tried their hands at Kedgeree that day!

the late Peter Bull
Ex-RNVR Officer, publisher,
writer, actor and especially famous
for his large collection of Teddy Bears

*Sadly, this recipe with
his accompanying letter
was the last letter
Peter Bull wrote before he died*

POACHED SALMON STEAKS
with a soured cream dressing

1. Mix 1 pint soured cream, a handful of parsley and the juice of a lemon
2. Cut salmon into ½inch thick steaks
3. Mix together ½ pint dry white wine, 2 bay leaves, 1 sliced lemon, five peppercorns, 2 tbs chopped spring onion. Boil quickly. Once boiled add steaks, and add water to liquid until it covers steaks.
4. Simmer for about 2 minutes
5. Leave to stand while you arrange iceberg lettuce on the plates
6. Put steaks on lettuce and fill the gaps in the steaks with large prawns
7. Pour dressing over prawns and lettuce — leaving the salmon uncovered.

Peter Watts,
Chef and Joint Proprietor
Bullers Arms, Chagford

SOLE au CITRON VERT

Serves 2

4 fillets of sole
3 tbs butter
2 tbs soured cream
2 carrots
1 lime (or lemon)
2 tsp sugar
1 courgette
Salt and pepper
A few French beans

1. Cut carrots in julienne strips and cook for 10 mins
2. Cut beans and courgettes julienne and cook
3. Cook goujons of sole in butter until lightly brown
   Take out of pan
4. Add juice of lime to butter in pan, with
   2 tbs soured cream. Stir
5. Add 1 tbs more of soured cream if not tasty enough
6. Add fish and more butter on a high heat
7. Add candied lime peel
8. Serve on julienne of vegetables.

Hélène Boeuf
Charleroi, Belgium

TROUT with SORREL SAUCE

Go out and catch a trout . . . or failing that, buy some from your fishmonger...or if you are feeling rich, some sea-trout or salmon.

1. Butter some foil and put in the cleaned fish, more butter and 1 tbs dry white wine or vermouth
2. Cook at Gas Mark 4 for 25—30 mins.
3. Meanwhile make sauce —
    Cook a few handfuls of sorrel in a knob of butter and water left on leaves after washing
4. Stir to reduce to a purée
5. When fish is cooked, remove skin
6. Add double cream to sorrel purée, and wine and buttery liquid from foil
7. Serve fish on *top* of sauce
8. Accompany with new potatoes.

The contrast of pink fish and marbled green sauce has eye appeal.

Geoff Nyburg
London

Poultry

APPLE STUFFED DUCK

A freshly plucked duck of
about 5 lbs is right for this
recipe and is enough for two
hungry people

1. Take ¼ pint of rough cider and mix it with onion, sage and wholemeal breadcrumbs
2. Chop duck's liver roughly and fry in butter until browned. Add this to stuffing with a chopped Bramley apple and seasoning to taste
3. Stuff the duck and stitch it
4. Bake on a rack in a medium oven for about 90 minutes
5. Drain off fat and then pour over ½ pint of cider. Return to the oven for another 30 minutes, basting every 10 minutes or so. You may have to turn the oven up at this stage to make the skin crisp.

A sauce can be made from the remaining juices and cider — but I prefer to eat the duck on its own.

Peter Watts,
Chef and Joint Proprietor,
Bullers Arms,
Chagford

BRANDY CHICKEN with SCAMPI

Serves 4

4 fresh chicken breasts
2 oz butter
1 rounded tsp prepared English mustard
2 tbs brandy
1 oz cornflour
8 oz frozen scampi (thawed)
Salt and pepper
½ pint single cream
4 oz fresh or frozen prawns

1. Make slight cuts in each chicken breast
2. Rub a little mustard on to them
3. Gently melt butter in a saucepan, and fry chicken on all sides until cooked through — about 20 mins
4. Add scampi and cook for 7 minutes
5. Pour in brandy and set it alight
6. Remove from heat. After 20 seconds add 6tbs water
7. Return to heat and stir well
8. Mix cornflour with 1/3rd of the cream
9. Remove pan from heat and stir in blended cornflour, remaining cream and salt and pepper
10. Reheat gently; do NOT let it BOIL
11. When mixture thickens, add prawns and heat for 1 minute. Keep warm
12. Serve with savoury rice.

Lt-General Michael Matthews C.B.
CinC Royal Engineers

CHARTER PIE — My favourite recipe

"Borrowed" from Jane Grigson who "borrowed" it from someone else.

A grand variation of the Cornish pasty or leek pie. It can be eaten hot or cold since the juices set to a white jelly flecked with parsley.

> *2 x 3lb chicken, jointed*
> *Seasoned flour*
> *Large onion, chopped*
> *4 oz butter*
> *3 oz bunch parsley*
> *1 fine leek or 6 spring onions*
> *¼ pint each milk and single cream*
> *½ pint double cream*
> *Salt and pepper*
> *Rich shortcrust pastry*

Roll chicken in flour. Soften onion in half the butter, season and put into a large pie dish. Add rest of butter to pan and, when hot, brown chicken lightly to a nice gold. Put on top of onions in a single layer. Chop parsley and white part of leek or all spring onions (except any roots). Simmer for 3 minutes in milk and single cream. Add salt and pepper. Pour over chicken and add a third of the double cream.

Cover with pastry in usual way, making a good central hole that will later take a small kitchen funnel. Run a pastry brush round the inside of the single cream pot and brush over the pastry (or use egg glaze). Bake at 200C (425F) Gas 7 for about 20 minutes, until pastry begins to colour. Then lower to 180C (350F) Gas 4 and leave until chicken is cooked, testing it through the central hole with a larding needle or skewer.

Bring the remainder of the cream to boiling point and pour it in through the hole, using a funnel or rolled-up card.

Bev Puxley,
Head of Professional Cookery
Westminster Catering College,
London

CHICKEN CORONATION SALAD

A tasty way to use up left over
chicken, ham or turkey

½lb chicken
¼ pint mayonnaise
4 sticks celery
1 small tin apricots
¼lb grapes
1 tsp curry powder
Salt and pepper

1. Roughly chop celery, chicken and apricots.
   Halve and pip grapes
2. Put mayonnaise into a bowl and thin it down to
   a "coating" consistency with the juice from the
   apricots
3. Season to taste with the salt, pepper and
   curry powder
4. Add all other ingredients to the mayonnaise,
   holding back a few apricots and grapes for the
   garnish, and mix thoroughly
5. Serve with a crisp green salad.

N.B. *HAM CORONATION goes well with
pineapple instead of apricots.*

Jules Lloyd,
Chef on board
charter yacht
"Lady Jenny III"

CHICKEN LUCY

4 chicken portions
1 small onion
2 small tomatoes
1 small green pepper
2 oz mushrooms
4 pancakes
1 lb frozen puff pastry
Cooking oil

1. Slice onion, tomatoes, green pepper and mushrooms
2. Sauté gently in a little cooking oil for about 10 minutes
3. Spoon the mixture over each chicken portion and wrap a pancake around each one
4. Roll out puff pastry and wrap tightly round each chicken portion and seal
5. Place in greased oven proof dish and cook in a fairly hot oven, gas Mark 6 for 25—30 minutes.

Serve with new potatoes and
fresh asparagus.

Mike Lucy
Catering Manager of
Queen's Park Rangers
London

CHICKEN ROULADES

Serves 4

4 chicken breasts, boned and skinned
4 slices lean ham
3 oz butter
5 oz Gruyère cheese, grated
1 tbs oil
4 oz white breadcrumbs
2 rosemary sprigs
2 beaten eggs

1. Beat chicken breasts flat.
   Cut slice of ham in half and place 2 halves on the chicken breast—folding so that the ham does not overlap edges.
   Repeat with rest of ham and chicken
2. Take 3 oz cheese and divide it between chicken breasts, sprinkling it over the ham
3. Place rosemary on top of each chicken breast and roll up neatly. Secure with a cocktail stick.
   Mix remaining cheese with breadcrumbs
4. Brush each roulade with egg, then coat with breadcrumb mixture. Pat mixture firmly on to roulades
5. Melt butter and oil in pan. Fry roulades quickly until browned all over, then reduce heat and cook slowly for 15 minutes approx
6. Drain on kitchen paper and remove cocktail sticks
   Serve plain or with tomato sauce
   Garnish with sprigs of rosemary and tomato wedges and salad or vegetables.

Josephine Blake,
National Theatre

69

FAISAN DIABLE

1 pheasant
1 pint cream
1 tsp mustard
1 tsp Harvey's sauce
1 tsp Worcester sauce
Seasoning

1. Roast the pheasant
2. Whip the cream with all the other ingredients and put it aside
3. Cut up pheasant and put it in an ovenproof dish
4. Pour over the cream sauce
5. Brown under the grill but do *NOT* let it *BOIL*.

Mushrooms sautéed in butter can be added to the cream sauce if wished.

Dame Nancy Snagge D.B.E.
Director of W.R.A.F. 1950–56
ADC to Her Majesty the Queen

FRICASSÉE of CHICKEN and HAM

1 lb cooked chicken or turkey
½lb cooked ham or grilled bacon
½ lb mushrooms
Chicken stock
2½ oz butter
1 oz flour
Milk
Tomatoes
Salt and pepper

1. Melt butter in pan. Add flour and stir. Add milk and stock. (A little white wine may be added)
2. Fry mushrooms in some butter
3. Add ham and chicken and mushrooms to sauce
4. Slice tomatoes and cook
5. Transfer to dish and decorate with tomatoes.

**Sir Peter Mills,
MP for West Devon**

HERBY CHICKEN

Serves 4

4 chicken pieces
2 oz melted butter
1 pkt plain crisps — crushed
4 oz grated cheese
Pinch garlic powder
1 tbs chopped fresh tarragon
Salt and black pepper

1. Coat chicken pieces with half the melted butter
2. Mix together the crisps, cheese, garlic powder, tarragon, salt and pepper
3. Press this mixture into the chicken and arrange in a baking dish
4. Sprinkle with remaining butter
5. Bake in a preheated oven at 350°F for 45 minutes to 1 hour, or unti chicken is cooked
6. Serve hot.

Throwleigh W.I.
Devon

HUNGARIAN CHICKEN

1 roasting chicken
2 large onions
1 tbs lard
2 cups stock
3 tsp paprika
2 green peppers
2 large tomatoes or 1 tin (drained)
2 tbs cream
1 dsp flour
Salt and pepper
Rice

1. Cut chicken into pieces and flour well
2. Chop onions
3. Melt lard and fry onions till soft
4. Sprinkle in paprika, mix and cook for a few minutes
5. Add chicken pieces ad stock and salt
6. Bring to boil, stirring occasionally, and simmer 40 minutes
7. Add sliced tomatoes, peppers and chopped chicken livers and simmer 15 mintues
8. Lift out chicken pieces and arrange in dish Surround with rice
9. Blend flour in mixture in pan
   Boil for 3 minutes
   Blend in cream — off the heat —
   Pour over chicken and serve.

Sheelagh Knox,
Well Farm,
Throwleigh, Devon

PIGEONS in ELDERBERRY WINE

Serves 4

"First, shoot your pigeons — and make your wine! Of course, any red wine will do, but if you make your own, the flavour is delicious and the wine is cheap!"

4 pigeons, plucked and drawn
Seasoned flour
2 large sliced onions — or button onions
2 oz butter
Bay leaf
Bacon rinds
Marjoram
Basil
Parsley
½ pint wine
½ pint stock or water
Bacon rolls for serving

1. Melt butter in large deep pan
2. Toss pigeons in plastic bag containing seasoned flour
3. Brown pigeons in butter, then onions
4. Throw over the wine, at a good heat
5. Add stock, herbs, bay leaf, bacon rinds
   Reduce heat and simmer for 2—3 hours or until pigeons are tender
6. Remove pigeons and place on serving dish
7. Sauce should be ready to pour over them
   Adjust seasoning and thickening
8. Garnish with bacon rolls.

N.B.   *A pressure cooker will cook this dish*
        in half an hour.

Elizabeth Haughton
Chagford

74

QUICK CHICKEN PILAU

Serves 2

2 chicken joints — diced
1 oz margarine
1 large onion, peeled and chopped
8 oz long grain rice
1 pint chicken stock
2 oz sultanas
1 tsp basil
1 tsp tomato purée
Salt and pepper

1. Sweat onion in butter
2. Add rice, stock and seasonings
3. Bring to boil. Cover and simmer for 20 minutes until liquid has been absorbed
4. Remove lid and add sultanas and chicken
5. Cook gently for about 5 minutes

Serve at once.

Jean Nyburg

SPICY CHICKEN

6 chicken joints
2½ oz butter
1 lemon
1 medium onion
2 oz soft brown sugar
1 level tbs cornflour
2 tsp made mustard
1 tsp Worcester sauce
Salt and pepper
½ pint water
1 x 2½ oz tin tomato purée

1. Heat 2 oz butter in large frying pan. Add chicken, and brown on all sides
2. Place in casserole. Add ½ lemon, sliced
3. Add rest of butter to frying pan and sweat onion
4. Put sugar, cornflour, mustard, Worcester sauce, salt, pepper, juice of ½ lemon, tomato purée and water in a basin and mix
5. Add to onion in frying pan. Stir and bring to boil
6. Simmer for a few minutes, and then pour over the chicken pieces
7. Cover and place in centre of moderate oven/Gas Mark 4/ for one hour
8. Spoon chicken pieces and sauce onto a serving dish and take to table.

Elizabeth Counsell
National Theatre

Meat

"and all that TRIPE"

First get a Rayburn!
Set at 300° F

    Place in a covered dish:
    1lb tripe per serving
    1 onion per serving
    1 cup milk per serving

Cut tripe to bite size pieces and
onion in quarters
Garnish with 20 peppercorns and
8 bay leaves
Completely forget for 3—6 hours
Enjoy with potatoes and something
green or red for colour.

Ron Rankin,
Lower Park,
Gidleigh, Devon

BARBECUE SPARE RIBS

Serves 4

4lb pork spare ribs — jointed
1 small can of crushed yellow bean sauce
(available from Chinese supermarkets or
Sharwoods)
1—2 cloves garlic
3 tbs soya sauce
3 tbs sugar
Crushed ginger to taste

1. Put all ingredients, except ribs, in a saucepan and heat until well combined
2. Pour sauce over the ribs and allow to marinate for 3—4 hours or overnight
3. Cook in a preheated oven 350°F for 30 minutes
4. Remove, turn ribs, baste with marinade and return to oven for 40 minutes more, then serve.

They can be finished off on a charcoal grill with a honey glaze if desired.

Rt Hon. The Earl of Lichfield F.I.I.P., F.R.P.S.

BEEF CURRY

from THAILAND

Best made 1—2 days in advance and reheated.
Make plenty — It freezes well.

> 2lb stewing beef
> 2 onions
> 3 cloves garlic
> 2 tbs curry paste
> 4—6 tbs cooking oil
> 1 tsp salt
> 1 tbs dessicated coconut
> 2 tbs sugar
> 1—2 tsp lemon juice
> 2 tomatoes
> ½ pint milk

1. Trim fat from meat — cut into cubes
2. Peel and slice onions, crush garlic and fry in hot oil
   Add coconut
3. Reduce heat and cook 2—3 minutes, when mixture
   will give off a nutty aroma
4. Add curry paste, cook further 2—3 minutes
5. Add cubed meat, leave over gentle heat 5—7 mins
   till meat is sealed on all sides
6. Stir in sugar, salt, lemon juice and
   coarsely chopped tomatoes
7. Slowly add milk to cover meat, stirring throughout
   *Add milk slowly, so that coconut will combine and
   thicken curry. When added too quickly, sauce tends
   to be thin and liquid.*

Cover and simmer 2½—3 hours.
If curry is too hot — add more sugar.

Daphne Jackson,
Murchington, Devon

BOTHAM'S BOLOGNESE 'OWZAT

Spaghetti Bolognese   Serves 4

2 tbs oil
2 tsp sugar
250g lean minced beef
Salt and pepper
1 onion, peeled, sliced and chopped
1 bay leaf
A little water
1 x 379g can tomatoes
350g spaghetti
2 tbs tomato purée
25g butter
1 clove garlic, crushed
Parmesan cheese

1. Put oil into medium sized saucepan over moderate heat
2. Add mince and onion and brown for 5 minutes turning occasionally with a wooden spoon
3. Add tomatoes, purée, garlic, sugar and seasoning and bay leaf
4. Bring to the boil, stir, cover and simmer for 40 mins Add more water if mixture looks dry
5. After 20 mins, cook spaghetti for about 12 minutes
6. Drain spaghetti. Tip into warm bowl with butter and pepper. Toss
7. Pour meat sauce into a bowl and serve straight away with spaghetti and Parmesan cheese.

Ian Botham,
England cricketer

BRESSAOLA

" I have racked my brains and can't think of a single recipe. This is because I don't really think about food. I eat things when they are put in front of me, but I have never thought specifically about any particular dish.

I usually eat without noticing that I have done so, and unless I am on holiday in France or Italy, I tend to ignore food altogether.

The only dish which has consistently penetrated my fog of indifference requires no cooking at all. It is called *BRESSAOLA*.

It consists of extremely thin, almost transparent slices of smoked beef. You serve it with olive oil and lemon and its appearance is as nice as its taste.

It is like a gastronomic equivalent of:
   EATING STAINED GLASS WINDOWS!!"

**Jonathan Miller,
well-known for practically everything!**

82

CHUMP CHOPS for DINNER

2 chump chops
Flour for coating chops
2 tbs lemon juice
1 tbs brown sugar
1 tsp ground ginger

1. Flour chops and pour 2 tbs lemon juice over
2. Add 2 tsp ground ginger and 1 tbs brown sugar
3. Stir and pour over chops in a shallow dish
4. Leave for 2 hours or overnight, turning once or twice in sauce
5. Grill 8 minutes on both sides, basting with left-over marinade.

It is really delicious. Try it with either potatoes or rice and a green vegetable.

Adelaide Hall,
legendary Jazz singer

CORNISH PASTY

A real Cornish recipe from MOUSEHOLE

To make one large or 2 small pasties
SHORTCRUST PASTRY
4 oz flour
2 oz fat (½ margarine, ½ lard)
Pinch of salt
Water to mix to a firm dough
FILLING
Finely sliced potatoes, onion and swede
(all the same size)
4 oz lean beef, chuck steak or skirt is best
Cut into small pieces — do NOT mince!
Seasoning

1. Roll pastry into one or two rounds
2. Pile on potatoes, then onion and swede
   Season each layer according to taste

3. Place meat on top covered with a few slices of
   potato to prevent meat drying out
   A little beef dripping may be added if liked
4. Damp edges of pastry. Fold over and crimp edges
5. Bake at 425° F/Mark 7, for 15 minutes. Reduce to
   350° F/Mark 4 for another 30 mins.

NOTE: *The Cornish people crimp the pastry with the
left hand and fold over by right hand, forming a rope-
like effect on side of pastry. Some crimp the top of
the pastry and some the side. My mother-in-law (born
1884) was taught by her mother to crimp pastry on
the top — slit the side to let out steam and then draw
an initial on the corner of each pasty, so that each
person knew their own pasty. They were always such
large pasties that most people saved a corner for
supper!*

> Pauline Truscott,
> Chagford, Devon

EASY BAR B QUE RIBS

Spare ribs — pork or beef
Sazon stuffing or garlic or
your favourite seasoning
Salt and pepper
Your favourite Bar B Que Sauce
(Chita likes Hunt's Hickory Flavoured)

1. Place ribs in pot and cover with water
2. Add sazon or other seasoning, salt and pepper
3. Bring to the boil and reduce to simmer until meat is tender, 1—2 hours
4. Remove ribs from pot and place in baking pan
   Cover bottom of pan with liquid from pot
   Cover ribs with Bar B Que Sauce
5. Put in oven 350° F. Turn every ½ hour
6. Bake until meat falls off bone, 1—2 hours.

Serve with: baked beans
             maple syrup
             brown sugar
             mustard
   Combine these to taste and
   bake at 350° F for 1—1½ hours.

"Chita loves to combine easy things, add her own touches and it comes out tasting like she's been slaving all day over a hot stove!"

Chita Rivera,
famous Broadway star.
Just received a "TONY" award
for best actress in "THE RINK"

85

HACHEE

Dutch recipe

500g stewing steak
3 onions
150g half butter, half vet (margarine)
1 tbs flour
Pepper
1 bay leaf
3—4 tbs vinegar
2 cloves
1¼ pints water and stock cube or thinned gravy
Big pinch sugar

1. Cut meat into small cubes and sprinkle with salt
2. Fry meat cubes together with finely cut onions in hot vet and butter till nicely brown, in heavy casserole
3. Sprinkle with flour and stir till light brown
4. Add gravy stock, stirring all the time, with spices and vinegar
5. Finally add sugar and simmer for 2¼ hours on top of stove, stirring occasionally to prevent sticking
6. Serve with boiled potatoes and apple sauce, or mashed potatoes or rice.

**Marja Lee,
Costume designer
Chagford, Devon**

KIDNEYS with SHERRY

Cooking time 20—25 minutes Working time 10 minutes

2 calves' or pig's kidneys
Butter
3—4 mushrooms, sliced
1 glass fino sherry
1—2 large potatoes peeled and sliced
4—5 tablespoons stock
1 clove garlic, crushed or chopped
Salt and pepper

1. Prepare kidneys
2. Melt a little butter in a pan and sauté kidneys and sliced mushrooms for a few minutes
3. Pour over the sherry and bring to the boil
4. Boil rapidly until the liquid is reduced to half
5. Add the stock, the crushed garlic and the peeled and sliced potato
6. Season with salt and pepper
7. Cover and simmer gently for a further 10—15 min.

Serving suggestion: Serve with a side salad and some French bread to mop up the juice.

Lynda Goetz,
from her book
"Top Level Cookery for Two"
published by New English Library

LAMB CHOPS PAPRIKA

Serves 2

4 small lamb chops
1 medium onion
2 oz butter
½lb tomatoes
1 small carton yoghurt
2 heaped tsp paprika
Bay leaf

1. Use metal casserole with lid
2. Chop onion and fry in butter
3. Cut fat off chops
4. Fry chops in butter and onions, then remove from pan to plate
5. Skin and chop tomatoes and add to onions with seasoning and bay leaf
6. Cook for a few minutes, stirring
7. Return chops to casserole and turn them over in the sauce
8. Put lid on and simmer for 1 hour or cook in oven at 325°F for 1½ hours
9. Add yoghurt before serving and stir in lightly.

Sir Cecil Clothier K.C.B., Q.C.
The Ombudsman

LAMB'S HEARTS

Cooking time 30—35 mins.   Working time 15—20 mins.

2 large carrots
1 large or 2 medium onions
2 lambs' hearts
1 tbs olive oil
Knob of butter
6—7 tbs water
Juice of ½ lemon
Pinch of ground coriander
Pinch of cumin seeds
Pinch of rosemary
Salt and pepper

1. Slice the carrots and chop the onions
2. Cut the hearts into cubes or slices
3. Heat the oil and butter in a pan and sauté the vegetables and the hearts for 5 minutes. Cover the pan and continue cooking for a further 5 minutes over a gentle heat
4. Add the water, lemon juice, coriander, cumin and rosemary
5. Season, then re-cover and cook gently for a further 20 minutes

Do make sure if your pan lid is not close-fitting that the water does not all evaporate! Add a little extra water if necessary.

This dish does not have a lot of sauce. If you prefer something less dry, it is better to use ¼ litre (½ pint) of stock to add a little flavour rather than just using water.

Serving suggestions: Serve this with plain boiled or saffron rice.

Lynda Goetz,
from her book
"Top Level Cookery for Two"
published by New English Library

89

LAMB'S KIDNEYS in Butter & Mustard Sauce

Serves 2

6 lamb's kidneys
(can be more or less depending on your appetite)
Knob of butter
1 tbs finely chopped spring onions
or ordinary onions
1/3rd cup dry white wine
1 tbs butter
1 tbs Dijon mustard
Salt, pepper and chopped parsley

1. Melt butter in shallow casserole or deep frying pan
2. Add prepared kidneys. Cook on both sides for 10 minutes until pink inside and cooked outside Remove to warm plate
3. Add onions to butter in casserole or pan and cook for 1 minute
4. Add white wine and boil — while scraping up the bits on the bottom of the casserole!
5. Take off heat and add mustard and butter Season to taste
6. Slice kidneys ¼ inch thick at slight angle and add to casserole
7. Heat over a low heat for a couple of minutes to heat kidneys through
8. Add sprinkle of parsley and serve with boiled rice.

Rt Hon Dr David Owen MP,
Leader of S.D.P.

90

LAMB SHREWSBURY

2 lamb chops for each person
1 tbs flour
½ pint stock
4 tbs redcurrant jelly
2 tbs Worcester sauce
Juice of 1 lemon
Fat for frying
¼lb mushrooms
Pinch ground nutmeg
Freshly milled pepper
Chopped parsley

1. Trim chops
2. Brown on both sides in fat
3. Place in dish with mushrooms
4. Add Worcester sauce, redcurrant jelly and lemon juice
5. Stir over low heat until blended (may help to whisk)
6. Add flour to fat in frying pan, stir in melted jelly and enough stock to make gravy
7. Pour over chops, cover and cook 1½ hours in a moderate oven.

   Serve sprinkled with chopped parsley.

Naomi Barker,
Chagford, Devon

"MONKEY GLAND" STEAK

Served at Adelphi Hotel,
Liverpool in the 1930s

Fillet steak
Dijon mustard
Pepper
Salt
Worcester sauce
Parsley

1. Flatten steak and season with salt and pepper
   Smear with mustard
2. Sweat onions in butter and then add steak
3. When steak is cooked, add a dash of Worcester sauce
4. Add brandy and set alight
5. Put lid on pan to put out flame
6. Garnish with parsley

Silvano Spiro
Liverpool

PIGS' KIDNEYS with MUSHROOMS, PEPPERS and WHITE WINE

Cooking time 30 minutes Working time 10—15 minutes plus 1 hour soaking

2 pigs' kidneys
25g (1 oz) butter
2 small rashers bacon, diced
3—4 mushrooms, sliced
1 sweet red pepper, sliced
1 glass white wine
4 tbs meat stock
Chopped parsley
Bouquet garni
Salt and pepper

1. Soak the kidneys in warm salted water for 1 hour Cut them transversally into slices about ½ in thick.
2. Melt the butter in a saucepan. Add the diced bacon and the kidneys and cook gently for 1 minute
3. Add the sliced mushrooms and red pepper. Fry for a few minutes and then turn up the heat, add the wine and allow it to bubble for a minute or two
4. Lower the heat, add the remaining ingredients and simmer gently, covered, for 15 minutes.

Serving suggestion: Serve sprinkled with parsley on a bed of rice or with Mousseline potatoes.

Lynda Goetz,
from her book
"Top Level Cookery for Two"
published by New English Library

PLANKED STEAK or SURF 'n' TURF

1. **To prepare plank**
   Rub hollow with dripping, oil or butter, and then with garlic, sprinkle with herbs, fresh if possible. Put plank in hot oven, regulo 8 or 450°F. After 30 minutes, when plank is hot — add the meat.

2. **The Meat**
   Use this method for cooking fillet, sirloin or rump steak, sausages, chops or even hamburgers.

   Place meat in hollow in plank, and put a little oil or butter on meat.
   Place in hot oven (as above)
   Turn meat after 5 minutes and continue cooking for another 15 minutes or to taste.

   If meat is not top quality, marinate it for a few hours or overnight.

   MARINADE — Worcester sauce, oil, salt, pepper and some herbs.

3. **To decorate and serve**
   Remove plank from oven
   Put a pat of savoury butter on top of meat to melt, and a small portion of boursin cheese, herb and garlic or pepper flavours, if liked.
   To add colour, put some fresh tomatoes and watercress around the meat.
   The plank can then be taken to the table for serving.

N.B. Put plank on a heat resistant mat.

4. **For Surf 'n' Turf**
   In addition to above, you will need some Dublin Bay prawns, shelled and tossed in butter and served on top of the meat with butter and cheese as above. Add wedges of lemon.

continued on next page

THE PLANK

Wood, seasoned or kilned oil, 12" x 14" and 2" to 3" thick. With a gouge, make a hollow in the middle to a depth of 1" to 1½" and leaving a rim of 1" round the sides — working from sides to middle. To proof — rub with oil or dripping and garlic and sprinkle with herbs. Put in a cool oven and gently raise heat to regulo 6 or 400°F. Leaving at this heat for 30 minutes.

Turn off oven and let plank cool inside. It should now be ready for use. If the wood cracks a little don't worry.

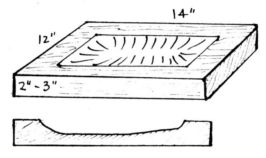

N.B. After cooking, when the plank is cool, the herbs and garlic should be wiped off with the kitchen paper.

DO NOT WASH THE PLANK —
IT MAY MAKE THE WOOD CRACK

The idea is that the flavours and juices will seep into the wood and be given up to the meat with each cooking.

Donny McLeod,
Pebble Mill at One
BBC TV

PRESSED BEEF

3lb piece of beef
Mixed spice
Carrots
Onions
Brown sugar
Garlic
Gelatine
Salt

1. Soak meat overnight in a bowl of water with
   4—5 tbs salt
2. Heat sufficient water in a saucepan to cover meat
   Add 1 tbs mixed spice,
   1 tsp brown sugar
   1 tbs vinegar and a few
   carrots and onions
3. Push 2 pieces garlic in the meat and drop into
   saucepan, when water is hot but not boiling
4. Simmer gently until meat is tender but not ragged
   Carefully remove garlic and place meat in a tin or
   basin to fit closely
5. Measure out ¼ pint beef stock
   Mix 1 level dsp gelatine with a little of this —
   and then add remainder
6. Pour over meat to cover lightly
   Shake gently to fill up crevices
7. Cover with greaseproof paper and a plate
   Put weight on top
   Leave till cold. Turn out.

This can be made with brisket if you like fat —
but we use topside.

General and Mrs Walkey
Chagford, Devon

RABBIT STEW with GREEN BEANS

Serves 4

8 average rabbit joints
(middle, back and hind legs are best)
4 oz shin beef, coarsely chopped
2 large onions
1 clove garlic — crushed
Any root vegetables you may happen to
have around — potato, carrot, leek, swede or
turnip

1. Brown rabbit joints and beef swiftly in a little hot fat
   Beef or bacon fat is best, but any high grade
   cooking oil will do
2. Place on one side and soften onions, coarsely
   chopped, in remaining fat
3. Put meat and onions in a large casserole, add
   vegetables, coarsely chopped, and garlic
   Sprinkle with freshly ground black pepper and a
   little salt. Cover with boiling water
4. Cover casserole and cook in moderate oven for at
   least 2 hours (3 is better!)
5. Serve with finely sliced green beans.

Sir Larry Lamb,
Editor of the Daily Express

ROGHAN GOSH

2lb chuck beef or lean lamb
1 small tin tomatoes
1 chopped onion
2" fresh ginger — peeled and crushed
6 tbs plain yoghurt
2 cloves garlic — crushed
1 tsp turmeric
1 tsp ground coriander
1½ tsp ground cumin
½ tsp cinnamon
¼ tsp chilli powder
6 tbs oil

1. Heat oil and fry onions and garlic until slightly browned
2. Add meat and brown
3. Remove onions and meat from pan
4. Cook spices for 30 seconds, then add meat, onions, yoghurt and tomatoes
5. Cook at Gas Mark 4/350° F/180° C for about 1 hour or until meat is tender
6. Serve with plain, boiled rice, poppadoms, chappattis or naan bread, mango chutney and a green vegetable salad.

This is an introduction — an Indian family will have its own combination of spices. If you add more chilli powder it will be hotter — but it is up to you!

Most of these spices can be found in supermarkets. If you can't find them all, don't worry — but don't forget the yoghurt.

**Rt Hon. Neil Kinnock MP
Leader of the Labour Party**

SAUSAGEMEAT TART

8 oz shortcrust pastry
2 oz pitted black olives
½ lb pork sausagemeat
1 tsp mixed herbs
4 tbs tomato purée
1 small onion
Seasoning

1. Make 8 oz short crust pastry
2. Take half and cover 7—8 inch pie plate — lightly greased
3. Thinly dice ½lb fresh mushrooms and 1 small onion. Fry for 3 minutes
4. Add sausagemeat, olives, purée, mixed herbs and seasoning
5. Fry for 5 minutes and remove excess fat
6. Put filling into pie dish and cover with remaining pastry making 2 slits in centre
   Brush with milk and place in oven at 400°F for about 35—40 minutes.

Monica Dell
Internationally known Singer

SINGAPORE MINCE

Serves 4

2lb minced chuck steak
4 oz tomato purée
½lb onions
2 pts beef stock
½lb tomatoes
Pinch of basil
½ oz ground cumin
½ oz garam masala
½lb carrots
½ green pepper
½ red pepper
Salt and pepper

1. Finely dice onion. De-seed and dice red and green peppers. Peel carrots and cut into rounds
2. Put mince in thick-bottomed saucepan with onions peppers and carrots and stir over a medium heat
3. Meanwhile skin and de-seed the tomatoes, and chop flesh into dice
4. Allow mince to cook for about 15 minutes — stirring to ensure there are no lumps of meat
5. Stir in tomato purée, cumin and basil
   Then add stock
6. Pull pan to side of stove and simmer for about 45 minutes, stirring occasionally
7. Correct seasoning and add garam masala.

Nick Daymond,
Grand Metropolitan Super Chef
of S.E. England

SQUAB PASTIES

Traditional

Batch cooking/Freezing

1½lb cooked lamb (breast + lean shoulder)
1½lb cooking apples
3 onions
3 tbs sugar
2lb shortcrust pastry
Salt and pepper

1. Roast meat slowly in covered pan
2. Remove all bone and chop lean and
   fat meat together
3. Chop apples (skinned) and onions into small pieces
   and add with sugar and seasoning to meat
4. Roll out pastry and use a saucer to cut circles
   Fill with mixture, moisten edges and bake pasties
   in hot oven until pastry is cooked.

Sheelagh Knox,
Well Farm,
Throwleigh, Devon

STUFFED SHEEP'S HEARTS

2 or 3 hearts according to size
1lb meat for three people

1. Prepare by cutting out coarse tubes and excess fat
2. Wash in salted water
3. Make stuffing of orange, basil and anchovy —or—
   basil, apple mint and prune — and sew up with
   coarse white thread
4. Put in a baking tin with about ½ pint of good stock
5. Cover with foil or buttered paper
6. Bake for 1½—2 hours and keep well basted
7. Serve with redcurrant jelly, simple gravy,
   baked potatoes in their jackets and green beans.

Tommy Steele,
Famous Stage Star

STUFFED VINE LEAVES

Egyptian

1. Remove thick stems from several vine leaves
2. Place about a dessertspoonful of filling —
   mince with rice, cheese, ham or leftovers — and
   wrap the leaf neatly round it — tying it with cotton
3. Place them side by side in a fireproof dish with a
   little stock
4. Cover and cook in the oven till the leaves are tender
   — about 15 minutes.

Clementia Raikes,
Linwood, Hants

VEAL CORDON BLEU

Serves 4

4 veal escalopes, unbeaten 6—7 oz each
4 slices Gruyère cheese
3 tbs cooking oil
¼ pint Madeira
4 slices lean cooked ham
2 oz butter
½ pint rich brown stock
Freshly ground black pepper

1. Beat out escalopes to ¼ inch thickness
2. Top each with a slice of ham, cut to fit
3. Cover half with slice of cheese, and fold escalopes in two. Secure with 2 cocktail sticks
4. Melt butter and oil in large frying pan, and fry escalopes on both sides
5. Reduce heat and cook for 6 minutes on each side until tender and golden brown
6. Add stock and Madeira and simmer 5 mins
7. Remove meat and keep hot on serving dish
8. Season juices with black pepper and boil rapidly to reduce
9. Remove cocktail sticks — pour juices over escalopes and serve.

Lt-General Matthews CB
C in C Royal Engineers

Vegetables and Vegetarian

AUBERGINES in SOY SAUCE

Kaji changatchi

4 medium aubergines
2 oz lean beef
1 onion, finely chopped
1 clove garlic, finely chopped
½ tsp vinegar
2 green onions cut in 1" lengths
Salt
3 tbs soy sauce
1 tsp sesame salt
1 tsp sesame oil
1½ tbs sugar
1 tbs water

1. Cut aubergines across in 3 pieces. Slit each piece twice through the centre without cutting through the ends

2. Sprinkle with salt and leave for 15 minutes, then drain
3. Mince beef and season with soy sauce, onion, garlic, sesame salt and oil
4. Stuff aubergine pieces with beef mixture, then put them in a pan and sprinkle with vinegar, sugar, green onions, water and remaining soy sauce
5. Bring to the boil and simmer gently until the liquid is almost evaporated

SERVE AT ROOM TEMPERATURE

N.B. *Sesame salt is prepared by heating sesame seeds gently in a strong pan until they turn brown and swell.*
Then pulverise in a mortar or liquidiser, with 1 tsp salt per cup of sesame seed.

Rt Rev Richard Rutt,
Bishop of Leicester

BAKED POTATO CAKE

A recipe from the Lizard Peninsula in Cornwall

2 large raw potatoes
¼ lb suet
About 3 oz flour,
   depending on size of potatoes

1. Cut potatoes into small pieces
2. Mix with suet and flour until moist enough to put in a greased tin
3. Bake in a moderate oven for ¾ hour, or until brown
4. Cut into slices and eat with a roast dinner.

Pauline Truscott,
Chagford, Devon

BEAN SALAD

American

1 tin cut green beans ⎫
1 tin yellow wax beans ⎬ all drained
1 tin red kidney beans ⎭
(variations — tinned peas, chick peas,
other tinned beans)
1 cup chopped celery
½ cup chopped green peppers
Medium sliced onion, separated into rings
2/3rd cup wine vinegar/or white vinegar
¾ cup sugar
½ cup salad oil

Combine all ingredients, refrigerate overnight. Keeps several days in refrigerator and improves with age.

Anne Seery,
Boulder, Colorado, USA

BUTTERSILK CARROTS

Serves 6

8 unpeeled carrots
3 oz margarine
Pinch of sugar
1 tsp lemon juice
Pinch of salt
Dash of pepper
Handful of chopped parsley

1. Cut carrots into very thin matchsticks
2. Put margarine and lemon juice into heavy frying pan, and heat over very low heat until margarine is melted
3. Add carrots, shake pan to coat each stick
   Cover tightly and sauté about 15 minutes, shaking pan often
4. When just tender crisp, sprinkle on salt, sugar and parsley.

Shake pan to mix and serve at once.

Ginny Graham-Fletcher,
London

CHILLI BEAN STEW

1 pint stock or water
8 oz kidney beans
4 oz diced swede
4 oz diced onion
4 oz sliced carrots
4 oz diced celery
4 oz sliced leeks
4 oz diced potatoes
1 tin peeled tomatoes
4 oz tomato purée
Seasoning
Butter or margarine
Chilli powder } *to taste*
Garlic

1. Soak beans overnight
    Prepare all vegetables and sweat in butter for 5 mins
    COOK BEANS for at least 10 minutes
2. Add tomato purée and seasoning
3. Roughly chop tomatoes and add to pan
4. Stir in stock
5. Finally add beans and simmer for 20 minutes
6. Correct seasoning and consistency.
        SERVE WITH LOTS OF FRESH
        CRUSTY BREAD!!

Nick Daymond,
Grand Metropolitan Super Chef
of S.E. England

CLEO'S ITALIAN SPINACH TART

Serves 6

Pastry:
½ lb flour
Generous pinch of salt
1 level tbs
   confectioners' sugar
5 oz softened butter
1 egg yolk
4 tbs cold water

Filling:
¾ lb frozen spinach
2 tbs butter
Salt and freshly gound
   black pepper
½ lb cottage cheese
3 eggs, lightly beaten
1 – 2 oz freshly grated
   Parmesan cheese
6 tbs heavy cream
Freshly grated nutmeg

Pastry:

Sieve flour, salt and sugar into a mixing bowl. Rub in the butter with the tips of fingers until mixture resembles fine bread crumbs. Do this very gently and lightly, or mixture will become greasy and heavy. Beat egg yolk, add cold water, sprinkle over dough and work in lightly with your fingers. Shape moist dough lightly into a flattened round. Wrap in plastic and leave in refrigerator for at least one hour to "ripen". If dough is too firm for handling, allow to stand at room temperature until it softens slightly. Then turn it on to a floured board and roll out as required. Line a pie tin with the pastry, fluting the edges and chill. Prick bottom with a fork and bake "blind" at 450° for about fifteen minutes, just long enough to set the crust without browning it. Allow to cool.

Filling:

Cook spinach with butter, add salt and freshly ground black pepper to taste. Drain thoroughly and then add cottage cheese with beaten eggs, grated Parmesan, cream, and nutmeg to taste.

Spread the mixture in pastry shell and bake the tart at 375° for thirty minutes, or until the crust is brown and the cheese custard mix has set.

Cleo Laine,
Singer Extraordinary

111

COCONUT RICE and GROUNDNUT SAUCE

East African

½—1 cup lightly roasted and
  finely minced peanuts
Garlic
Root ginger
¼ tsp (or more to taste) each of
Ground cumin
Coriander
Turmeric

1. Fry crushed garlic and ginger in a little hot oil
   Add spices and then minced nuts
   Mix well and cook for a few minutes
2. Gradually stir in sufficient water to make sauce-like
   consistency. Amount of water depends on quantity
   of nuts used. Simmer gently for a few minutes
   Serve with Coconut Rice and beans
   e.g. haricot beans, black eyed, kidney.
   To make rice — grate or grind in blender ½ coconut
   (without husk). Infuse in boiling water for 1 hour.
   Squeeze out minced coconut and use the water to
   boil the rice.
   Use slightly less water than the usual formula:
   1 cup rice, 2 cups water, since the coconut makes
   it more moist when finally cooked.

M Buhl-Nielsen,
Tanzania

112

COURGETTE CASSEROLE

"I enjoy doing vegetables in the oven to keep the stove free for sauces.

So here is a courgette casserole I often use with roast meat or fish."

> 8 cups diced courgettes
> 1 large onion
> 1 finely chopped green pepper
> ½ cup olive oil
> 1 cup stale bread crumbs
> 2 large eggs, beaten
> 1 cup sharp Cheddar
> 1 tsp dried basil or 1 tbs fresh basil
> Salt and pepper

1. In a bowl combine courgette, pepper, onion, breadcrumbs, Cheddar, oil, basil, eggs, salt & pepper
2. Transfer mixture to 13" x 9" baking dish and bake in a preheated oven 350°F for 45 minutes or until top is browned.

**Julia McKenzie,
One of our best-loved actresses**

GARLIC POTATOES ELISABETH

1. Peel and slice large potatoes into ¼ inch discs
2. Into a wide roasting tin, pour milk and water to a depth of ¼ inch.
   Season with salt, black pepper and a clove or two
3. Add 2 oz butter (preferably unsalted, otherwise cut down on salt seasoning)
   Heat gently, then stir to mix melted butter through the milk
4. Cover the bottom of the tin with the potato discs
5. Cook uncovered in a hot oven for 20 minutes
   Sprinkle with parsley before serving.

Dermot Walsh,
well-known star of
stage and TV

HERBY SPINACH PANCAKES

Basic pancake batter
1½ lb spinach, fresh or frozen
8 oz Boursin garlic/herb cheese
4 oz béchamel sauce

1. Make about 12 small, thin pancakes
2. Cook spinach and drain.
   Add the béchamel sauce and garlic cheese to the drained spinach
   If you have a mixer, put the mixture in it, and liquidise for ½ minute. Add salt, pepper and nutmeg
3. Fill each pancake with a little of the spinach mixture
   Fold pancakes into squares or triangles, place in a buttered ovenproof dish
4. Melt about 2 oz butter and pour over, sprinkle with Parmesan or Cheddar cheese, and put under grill to get really hot or into hot oven for 10 minutes.

These pancakes can be stuffed with a variety of mixtures:
Chopped ham and mornay sauce
Smoked haddock and chopped egg
Stuffed cabbage

When filling is dry, pour over a béchamel sauce flavoured with tomato and achovy.

Her Grace the Duchess of Somerset
Maiden Bradley, Wiltshire

115

KHITCHARI

6 oz mung beans	6 oz long grain rice
6 tomatoes or	3 potatoes, peeled and
1 x 14 oz can tomatoes	cut in large pieces
2 onions, chopped	3 tbs oil
4 cloves garlic	3 large carrots,
½ tsp turmeric	cut into chunks
½ tsp ground ginger	½ tsp garam masala
1½ pints water	1 tsp ground cumin
2 tbs lemon juice	Pinch chilli powder
Few cardamon pods	Salt to taste

1. Peel, chop onion, fry in oil for 5 minutes
2. Pick over and wash beans and rice
3. Add spices to onion in saucepan
4. Add tomatoes, potatoes, mung beans and rice
   Stir on heat for a few minutes
5. Stir in water. Bring to boil. Cover saucepan and cook gently for 45 minutes, until beans and rice are cooked
6. Take off heat, leave pan to stand 15 minutes to absorb remaining liquid
7. Add lemon juice and sea salt to taste, stirring carefully so as not to mash up rice and vegetables too much
8. Serve with mango chutney and garnish with fresh tomato rings.

Chris says he can happily eat this night after night. It is easy to make as the preparation is all at once — then it can be put on the stove and forgotten about.

It can be kept warm for latecomers without harm — just don't put in the lemon juice and salt until the last minute!

**Chris Bonington,
World Famous Climber**

LEEK and NOODLE CASSEROLE

Boil 350 grammes of wholemeal noodles in salted water, with a little oil, until soft, then drain.

Cut 4 or 5 leeks into ½'' pieces, wash, then sauté in a large pan with some oil and water.

Add a small amount of granulated vegetable stock and curry powder to give a very mild taste.
Cook until soft but not coloured.

Place in a casserole dish in alternate layers of leeks and noodles.

As a fifth layer, cover with grated cheese and pour over this some single cream.

Bake in a hot oven until crisp and golden — approximately 20 minutes.

HRH Prince Charles

LEEKS

How to make the most of

a leek

Use

1. White part as hot vegetable
2. Next 2 inches of green in salad
3. Remainder of green in soup.

LEEK FLAN

8 oz flour (4 oz wholewheat, 4 plain)
4 oz fat and butter
3 tbs water

1. Mix together, by hand, the fat and butter
   Add flour
2. Add water and mix in with a knife. Finish by hand
3. Leave to rest for 10 minutes
4. After rolling out leave for another 10 minutes
5. Put in 10" flan tin. Cook blind
   Prick bottom with a fork
   Cook at Mark 6 for 15 minutes. Cool
6. Cook 3 leeks in butter until soft
7. Cook bacon, 5 oz
8. Mix 2 eggs, salt and pepper and ¼ pint milk
9. Pour into flan case Mark 4 for 35 minutes.
   OPTIONAL *Grate some cheese over the top*
   before cooking

Jean Nyburg

THE QUAY.
EXETER

NACKERJACK

A large Devon Dumpling originally eaten by
Tin Miners with a vegetable stew.

Stew:
1 lb leeks
¾ lb potatoes
½ lb carrots
A parsnip
1½ pints chicken stock
Salt and pepper
Nackerjack:
8 oz SR flour
4 oz shredded suet
½ level tsp salt

Cut up all the vegetables
Add chicken stock
Season to taste
Put in a casserole dish
and cook at 400° F
(Mark 6) for 1 hour.

Mix together to form a
soft dough. Put on top
of stew as a 1" thick lid
Cook for 20—25 mins
at 400° F (Mark 6).

Jean Nyburg

POMMES EMBARRASSE

1. Put into a saucepan some butter,
   chopped onion, salt and pepper
2. Fry onion, then add tomato purée and stir in a
   little water
3. Cut into cubes the amount of potato you require
   and slowly boil in this mixture — stirring most of
   the time.
   If it gets too dry, add a little more purée and water
   — but do not make it too liquidy
4. Serve when almost dry.

VERY TASTY WITH STEAK

Diana Boddington M.B.E.
Internationally known
Stage Manager of the
National Theatre, Lyttleton Theatre,
and previously the Old Vic

120

POTATO SALAD

2 lb potatoes
Wine vinegar
Chives
French mustard
Salt
Lettuce
Tarragon
Olive oil/Sunflower oil
Pepper

1. Steam or boil potatoes in their skins
2. Meantime — rub salad bowl with garlic
3. Mix 1 heaped tsp of French mustard with
   1 fl oz wine vinegar
   4 fl oz olive oil or sunflower oil
4. Refresh potatoes
5. Peel and slice cooked potatoes
6. Blend thoroughly with French dressing
7. Leave to get cold, and decorate with
   lettuce, chopped chives and
   chopped tarragon leaves.

Margaret Barker,
York

SPINACH and WALNUTS

"Here is a lovely way of making
spinach a bit special"

1. Prepare and cook spinach in the usual way
2. When it is completely drained, put it in your
   liquidiser with a couple of handfuls of walnuts,
   (about 4 oz)
   Liquidise for 20 seconds
3. Pour in 3 fl oz of double cream and liquidise for
   about 5 seconds

   This gives the cream time to mix in with the spinach,
   but not totally, so that when you serve it, it has
   a slightly "marbled" effect.

   "It tastes good, too!"

Jules Lloyd,
Chef on board the charter yacht
"Lady Jenny III"

STUFFED AUBERGINES

4 large aubergines
2 onions, finely chopped
2 cloves garlic, crushed
Some stoned black olives
4–6 oz thinly sliced mushrooms
½ pint stock
4 large ripe tomatoes, skinned,
  seeded and chopped
2 tbs chopped parsley
1 tbs tomato purée
3 oz brown breadcrumbs
5–6 chopped anchovy fillets
3 oz grated Gruyère cheese
Marjoram, thyme, oregano

1. Cut aubergines in half, lengthwise
   Scoop out pulp leaving shells intact
   Salt and drain shells for 30 minutes
   Rinse and dry carefully
2. Fry onions, aubergine pulp and mushrooms gently in some butter till very soft
3. Add tomato, the purée, the herbs, garlic and stock, stirring well, and finally the anchovies and olives
4. Mix breadcrumbs, cheese and parsley, and add cooked tomato mixture to them
5. Paint skin of each halved aubergine with olive oil, and pile mixture into each half
6. Bake in a covered dish in a moderate oven until the shells have softened and are cooked through.

Yehudi Menuhin,
World Famous Violinist

123

WHITE CABBAGE in ONION SAUCE

"You will find this a great standby when vegetables are in short supply."

1 lb of onions (you can't make onion sauce without plenty of onions)
2 oz margarine
1 to 1½ oz flour
1 pint milk
4 cloves
4–6 oz white cabbage
Salt and pepper

1. Thinly slice 1 lb onions
   Soften onions in margarine (or butter if you want to be "HAUTE"!)
2. Throw the flour into the onions
   Then the salt and black pepper
   Stir for a few minutes
   Add cloves
   Heat milk
3. Add milk slowly and keep stirring until sauce begins to thicken — without burning!
   FIVE MINUTES BEFORE SERVING MEAL
   Stir the thinly shredded cabbage into the hot sauce and serve while it is still crisp and crunchy.

NOTE: *Fish out the cloves unless catering for relatives!!*

Arnold Nyburg D.S.C.
Chagford

Pickled !

APPLE CHUTNEY

4 lb windfall appies
1 lb sultanas
1 pint vinegar
1 tsp ground ginger
1 clove garlic
1 lb onions
1 lb soft brown sugar
1 tsp salt
½ tsp black pepper

Peel and core the apples,
chop roughly, peel and
chop onions. Put all ingredients in pan,
bring to the boil and boil uncovered until
the chutney is thick and brown, about 4 hours
Pot while hot.

**Penelope Keith,
Star of Stage and TV**

BULLER'S ARMS BEER MUSTARD

1. Buy from a delicatessen some black and white mustard seeds
2. Cover about ½ pint of seeds with about ¾ pint bitter beer and ¼ pint vinegar
3. Add to this :-   2 pinches mixed spice
                    2 pinches mixed herbs
                    ½ tsp of tabasco
   Leave covered for a week
   The mixture will swell to twice its original size
4. Liquidise to crush the seeds
   I prefer about ½ the seeds crushed, but this is a matter of personal taste.

This mixture gives a mild mustard
which is particularly good
with ham.

Peter Watts,
Bullers Arms,
Chagford

CHILI SAUCE (Sweet)

Canadian

30 large ripe tomatoes
8 medium onions
3 sweet green peppers
2 sweet red peppers
2 cups diced celery
2 cups cider vinegar
1½ tsp cinnamon
½ tsp cloves
¼ tsp ginger
2½ cups brown sugar
3 tbs salt
6 tbs mixed pickling spices (tied in bag)
Use only firm, ripe, bright red tomatoes

1. Scald, skin and cut them up into a large preserving pan
2. Peel and dice onions
3. Remove stems and seeds from peppers
   Cut into strips. Dice celery
4. Add to tomatoes. Add all other ingredients
5. Bring to rapid boil; simmer uncovered until thick — about 3 hours
6. Pour into sterile jars and seal at once.

YIELD: *Approximately 8 pints*

Not too spicy but pleasant with cold
meats or for Spanish omelettes.

Mary Rankin,
Gidleigh, Devon

MINT SAUCE to KEEP

½ pint vinegar
6 oz granulated sugar
1 teacupful finely
chopped mint

1. Measure vinegar and sugar into a saucepan
2. Stir over low heat to dissolve sugar
3. Bring to the boil, then draw off heat
4. Add chopped mint and allow to cool
5. Pour into clean screw-topped jar and seal.

N.B. *Sauce should be very thick.*

When using add more vinegar.

**Millicent Davies,
Chagford, Devon**

PICKLED SHALLOTS

Buy 1 lb shallots
Plant them in the garden in
February

Harvest in July/August

Leave in the sun for ages —
until ripe

Peel shallots under running water/
and or running eyes!

Put in a mixing bowl and cover with brine
Leave for 24 hours — or when you remember

In the meantime, boil as much
vinegar as you need

To each pint add a large
tbs of pickling spices
Boil for a minute
Leave to get cold.

Back to the shallots!
Wash them — Put in a colander to drain
Pack tightly in ½ gal jars
and cover with spiced vinegar.

Lock away from predatory friends
and relatives for 6 weeks.

Zelda Lambert,
Chagford, Devon

PICKLED WATERMELON RIND

Canadian

1½ quarts watermelon rind, diced
3 tbs salt
3 quarts water
4 cups brown sugar
1 cup cider vinegar
2 tbs mixed pickling spices
3 x 3" sticks cinnamon

1. Eat the pink flesh! Peel off green skin from rind
   Dice and measure — you should have 1½ quarts
2. Soak overnight in 1 qt water and 3 tbs salt
3. In the morning, drain and rinse; cover with
   1 quart cold water and simmer till tender;
   drain thoroughly
4. Make syrup of remaining quart of water, the sugar
   and vinegar. Add spices tied loosely in a bag
   Simmer 5 minutes
5. Add ½ the water melon rind cubes to the syrup
   Simmer, lightly covered, till clear
   (about 45 minutes)
6. Remove from syrup, place in sterile jars and add
   remaining half of raw cubes to the syrup
7. Again cook until transparent and place in sterile jars
   There should be enough syrup to fill jars.

Seal at once.

YIELD: *3 pint jars.*

Mary Rankin,
Gidleigh, Devon

131

PLUM CHUTNEY

2 lb dark plums
½ lb apples — chopped
1 lb seedless raisins
1 ½ lb dark brown sugar
2 onions — chopped
1 tbs salt
½ oz allspice
½ oz ground ginger
1½ pints malt vinegar
Few chillies　} *optional*
2 crushed cloves garlic }
WARNING: DO NOT USE A COPPER PAN

1. Put ½ pint vinegar and all the sugar in a bowl in a warm place. Also warm jam jars
2. Put stoned plums, chopped apples and onions, raisins and other ingredients in pan
   Cook thoroughly
3. Then add sugar and ½ pint vinegar
   Boil till set. Stir frequently
4. Pour into warmed jars and cover as for other chutneys. Jam covers are not suitable.

Flavour improves with keeping.

**Phyl Williams,
Chagford**

SWEET and SOUR CHUTNEY

¾ lb onions
½ lb drained canned pineapple
12 fl oz spiced vinegar
½ lb demerara sugar

1. Simmer chopped onions and pineapple in the vinegar until soft
2. Add sugar and boil up to ½ hour
If necessary thicken with 1 tsp cornflour.

Jill Mahan,
Chagford

SWEET CUCUMBER PICKLE

Makes 4 lb

2 lb cucumbers
2 large onions — peeled and sliced
2 oz salt
1 large green pepper, halved and deseeded

Syrup:
1 pint cider vinegar
1 lb soft brown sugar
½ level tsp ground turmeric
¼ level tsp ground cloves
1 level dsp mustard seed
½ level tsp celery seed

1. Wash cucumber but do not peel
   Slice thinly and put in a large mixing basin with onion, shredded green pepper and salt
   Mix well. Cover with plate and stand for 3 hours
2. Rinse vegetables in colander under cold running water. Drain well and put in large saucepan
   Add vinegar, bring to the boil and simmer for 20 minutes
3. Add sugar and spices, stir over low heat to dissolve sugar, bring to boil and draw pan off heat
4. Turn into large mixing basin and set aside until cold
5. Pour into jars and cover with screw tops.

SERVE WITH COLD MEATS, RAISED PIES
or CHEESE and BISCUITS

Jean Nyburg

134

Nearly Slimming Snacks

BACON, CHEESE and MARMITE SANDWICHES

Brown bread
Butter
Cheddar cheese (sliced)
Bacon (grilled)
Marmite

1. Grill the bacon, and whilst it is cooking butter 2 slices of brown bread
2. Lightly spread Marmite on one buttered slice and lay slices of Cheddar cheese on top of this until it covers the Marmite
3. When nicely grilled, cover the cheese with the sizzling bacon and then complete the sandwich by placing the second slice of buttered bread on top
4. Cut into quarters and eat immediately.

Steve Davis,
International Snooker Champion,
Essex

CHEESEY FRUIT SALAD

Great recipe for reluctant dieters!

½ lb green grapes
4 apples
Lettuce
Juice of a lemon
6 olives
1 oz sultanas
Pepper and salt
Carton of natural yoghurt
8 oz cottage cheese

Cut grapes
Remove all seeds
Cut apples into dice
Toss in lemon juice to
stop them browning

Mix all ingredients with yoghurt

Season

Serve on a bed of lettuce

Jean Nyburg

CHIP BUTTIES

This is a favourtie Wogan recipe —
or so he says!

Take two slices of fresh
crusty white bread

Fill with sizzling hot
freshly fried chips —
making sure the bread
is liberally spread
with butter

Add salt and pepper and
dressing to taste.

EAT!!

Terry Wogan,
Star of many a programme
on TV and Radio

CROQUE MONSIEUR NYBURG

Cover slices of toast with
slices of ham

Top with cheese

. . . GRILL . . .

Serve with poached egg on
top of cheese

*Known in the family as
"Eggy, Hammy, Cheesey, Toasty"*

**Arnold Nyburg,
Chagford**

EGGS BENEDICT

Serve
hot, poached eggs
on
thick slices of cooked ham
on
buttered crumpets

Cover with
hollandaise sauce

Top with
sliced truffles

Serve at once.

**Mary Rankin,
Gidleigh, Devon**

HAM SAVOURY

4 slices of bread
2 tbs mayonnaise
4 slices cooked ham
Made mustard
Chopped parsley
6 oz Cheddar
Paprika
4 tomatoes

1. Toast bread on each side and spread with mayonnaise
1. Cover each piece with a slice of ham, sliced tomato some made mustard and the cheese
3. Place under the grill until the cheese melts
4. Decorate with a sprinkle of paprika and chopped parsley

Accompanied by a glass of wine from the wine box in the fridge and all's well!

Jean Nyburg

THE PERFECT LUNCHEON for Elderly Authors

Take one slice of bread from a freshly baked loaf (not more than eighteen hours old and preferably brown but *not* wholemeal which has bits of gravel in it).

Place in electric toaster and activate switch.

Turn the slice of bread every 20 seconds. First upside down, then back to front, then upside down again, and so on. Wear gloves if fingers are sensitive.

When the slice is a golden-brown, the colour of a well-done potato crisp, remove and butter moderately. Use a rich country butter, slightly salted, and work right up to the edges of the crusts.

Slice a block of fresh, mild Cheddar cheese — preferably from East Anglia but some Devon cheese from the South West area is tolerable in an emergency—into pieces exactly 3/16 of an inch thick. Assemble these on the buttered surface so that the surface is exactly covered. In no circumstances should the cheese ever protrude beyond the perimeters of the toast. Nor should gaps be left so that toast is visible in the chinks between slices of cheese. Tweezers can be helpful in easing small wedges of cheese into gaps.

Carefully spread on top of the cheese a half tablespoonful of marmalade. Homemade, of course, rough-cut. Try to obtain navel oranges from the hill area eight miles north of Cadiz, the zest has a fluted aftertaste which compliments the confident and almost cocky flavour of the juice.

Pour yourself half a litre of dryish white Vouvray.
ENJOY!

Frank Muir,
Radio and TV personality

141

POACHED EGGS

*A little change for poaching
eggs for breakfast*

1. Let water boil in pan
2. Rub a little butter or margarine around the
   poaching cup to prevent sticking
3. If you have any left over cooked rice or peas,
   put one teaspoon in poaching cup, and add a
   little salt and black pepper
4. Let egg cook until lightly done.

**Adelaide Hall,
Legendary Jazz Singer**

QUICHE LORRAINE

Hot or cold dish — Freezes well

8in pastry case
4 lean bacon rashers
3 eggs
½ pint single cream
Salt and pepper
Tomatoes

1. Make pastry case
2. Fry bacon. Drain. Put in pastry dish
3. Beat eggs, add cream and seasoning and continue beating
4. Put on top of bacon, with sliced tomatoes on top
5. Bake at Gas Mark 4/350° F.

REHEAT FROM FROZEN

Serve with crisp, green salad.

Jean Nyburg

143

QUICK MACARONI CHEESE

Boil the macaroni in water till soft
Make a thin cheese sauce — about
1 oz flour to 1 pint of milk —
Add cheese and mustard to taste

Stir in the macaroni and pour
into a pie dish

Place in the oven for a minute till
the surface is firm
then place slices of tomato,
grated cheese and brown breadcrumbs on top
with a few knobs of butter

Place the dish in a baking tin of water and bake
just long enough to brown the top.

N.B. *The same method can be used to save time
when making rice pudding.*

Clementia Raikes,
Linwood, Hants

QUICK SUPPER DISH

Take small slices of cooked turkey or chicken and place a celery heart on top (tinned celery is very good for this dish).
Season with salt and black pepper.
Roll individual portions in slices of ham and place in a buttered dish.
Cover with a cheese sauce and sprinkle with Parmesan cheese.
Grill under a medium hot grill until golden brown and piping hot.
Serve with a jacket potato and grilled tomatoes
Garnish with parsley or watercress if so desired.

Marian Willett,
Glendarah Guest House,
Chagford

/

SALMON/TUNA and CUCUMBER QUICHE

8 inch pastry case
Tin of salmon or tuna
½ sliced cucumber
½ pint single cream
3 eggs
Salt and pepper
Pinch of cayenne
2 oz grated cheese

1. Prepare pastry case
2. Put fish in pastry case
3. Overlap slices of cucumber on fish
4. Beat eggs, cream and seasoning
5. Pour on to fish and cucumber
6. Sprinkle cheese on top
7. Bake 30—40 minutes at Gas Mark 4/350° F.

SERVE HOT or COLD

FREEZES WELL

TIP: *Put quiche tin on to a baking sheet*
for crisper pastry.

Jean Nyburg

SARDINE ROLLS

1 can sardines
Little vinegar
Pepper
Beaten egg
Cheese pastry

1. Put sardines on a flat plate
2. Remove tails
3. Sprinkle lightly with pepper and vinegar
4. Mash well with fork
5. Make pastry into an oblong
6. Cut in half lengthwise
7. Brush the long edges with water
8. Put the sardine mixture near the outer edge of
   each strip
   Roll up each strip so that the edge of the pastry is
   underneath
9. Cut into lengths — place on a baking sheet —
   Brush with egg and bake for 15 minutes at 400° F.
   Cheese Pastry:
   4 oz SR flour
   2 oz grated cheese
   1 tbs cold water
   Salt and pepper
   2 oz butter
   Yolk of egg.

Jean Nyburg

SCRAMBLED EGGS

If there is a shortage of eggs. . .

Add 1 tbs per person of
Boiled rice
or
Macaroni
or
Chopped kipper
or
Smoked mackerel
or
Smoked cod
or
any salt fish
to each serving of
delicious light, creamy
scrambled eggs.
DELICIOUS!

**Clementia Raikes,
Linwood, Hants**

Sir Oswald MUESLI

Muesli
Remains of last night's
fruit salad

This is a way of getting children to eat breakfast
On top of their bowl of cereal, add a face made out
of bits of fruit — grapes or raisins for eyes,
a peach slice for a mouth, a cherry for a nose —
that sort of thing.

If the family disapproves of Sir Oswald Muesli — you
can try David Frosties or Sir Shreddie Laker!

Richard Stilgoe,
TV presenter, writer and
"Starlight Express' lyricist

SPEAKER'S SPECIAL

Fry some bacon
Make some toast
Butter it
Cover with cheese
and sliced onion
GRILL

Lord Tonypandy,
formerly Mr. George Thomas,
much-loved Speaker of the
House of Commons

STUFFED APPLES

4 dessert apples
4 oz grated cheese
1 oz raisins
1 oz chopped walnuts
1 tsp lemon juice
2—3 tbs mayonnaise
Lettuce
Parsley to garnish

1. Cut apples vertically
   Remove core and some of the flesh
2. Add flesh to other ingredients
   (except lettuce and parsley)
   Mix together well
3. Divide mixture between apple halves and serve on a
   bed of lettuce
   Decorate with parsley.

IF SLIMMING:

Use cottage cheese instead of Cheddar. Flavour it
with a speck of garlic salt.

To ring the changes, use tomatoes or green
peppers or a 3" length of cucumber instead of
apples.

Georgina Roberts,
Worcester

SWEDISH PANCAKES with BACON

*"I had these in Chicago where there is
a large Swedish population, though I suspect
they are just American —
the pancakes, I mean!"*

1. Make pancakes
2. Fry — or better, grill lots of very thin
   crispy bacon and heat it on top of the pancakes
3. Pour over each a dollop of maple syrup.

HORRIBLE — BUT DELICIOUS!!

Paul Eddington,
National Theatre

TATTY CAKE

4 oz lard or suet
2 oz sugar
4 oz flour
8 oz potatoes
2 oz sultanas

1. Crumb fat and flour
2. Add other ingredients
3. Add a little milk if necessary, but the mixture should not be too wet
4. Press into sandwich tin and cook for ½ to ¾ hour.

TRADITIONAL DEVONSHIRE RECIPE

Throwleigh W.I.
Devon

TOMATO and CHEESE PANCAKES

Serves 4

1 oz grated cheese
2½ oz SR flour
1 egg
1 tsp dry mustard
1 pinch of salt
Onion powder or garlic to taste
A little milk
1—2 tomatoes

1. Mix all the ingredients, except the tomato, into a stiff batter
2. Drop spoonfuls into hot shallow fat
3. Place a slice of peeled tomato on to each one, with another spoonful of batter on top
4. Turn each over to brown the second side
5. Serve very hot, with a sprinkling of coarsely grated cheese mixed with Marmite on the top.

Clementia Raikes,
Linwood, Hants

NEWPORT. DYFED. WALES

WELSH RABBIT

An old recipe from South Wales

Butter
Cheese
Mustard
Beer

1. Melt butter over moderate heat
2. Add grated cheese and beer
3. Stir to avoid burning
4. Add mustard and heat till bubbling
5. Serve at once on buttered toast
6. Paprika or nutmeg can be added for a change.

Dilys Vivienne Jones,
Cardiff, S. Wales

FISHGUARD. S.WALES

WELSH RAREBIT

*This is most tasty with grated
Cheddar cheese, a little made up mustard
pepper and salt.*

1. Mix to a paste with beer or milk and a
    spot of Worcester sauce
2. Toast bread on one side only
3. Cover other side with the mixture generously and
    brown under a grill or in oven
4. Sprinkle with cayenne pepper if fancied

SERVE AT ONCE

Mrs Doreen Wray,
Chagford,
Devon

156

Ever so slightly fattening

ALMOND CRUNCH APPLES

1. Melt 2 oz butter in 4 tbs water
2. Add 2 oz sugar and 1 lb sliced cooking apples
3. Add 4 cloves, if liked
4. Cover and simmer gently until cooked
5. Turn into heatproof dish

Topping:
1. Place 1 oz flaked almonds and 2 oz demerara sugar in a pan and heat until almonds brown
2. Stir in 2 oz butter and melt
3. Remove from heat and stir in 4 oz crushed digestive biscuits
4. Cover apple mixture and bake 15 minutes at 350° F.

SERVE WITH CLOTTED CREAM

Mrs Judith Cosford,
Chagford, Devon

APPLE SLICES

Dessert Apples

Peel, core and slice thickly and evenly
Fry in plenty of butter till soft
and almost transparent
Remove them very gently to serving dish
Serve with whipped cream
Sprinkle well with soft brown sugar mixed
with powdered cinnamon.

**Mrs B.U.S. Cripps,
Chagford, Devon**

Teign Estuary.

BANANA CREAM DESSERT

Serves 3

3 bananas
2 tbs dry white wine
2 tbs caster sugar
2 tbs lemon juice
½ pint double cream

1. Liquidise bananas with wine and lemon juice
2. Whip cream fairly stiffly and fold into mixture
3. Serve in individual dishes or one serving bowl
4. Refrigerate for 10 minutes before serving.

Sheila Engelse,
New Malden

BANANA, RHUBARB & NUTTY GINGER

3—4 large ripe bananas
Small quantity cooked rhubarb or lemon juice
and rind
1 oz caster sugar
2 oz chopped walnuts
Ginger cake
2 oz butter

1. Grease soufflé dish
2. Layer sliced bananas with caster sugar, rhubarb or lemon juice and rind
3. Crumble ginger cake into melted butter in a saucepan and stir well
4. Chop walnuts and add to ginger mix
5. Pile on top of bananas
6. Bake at 375° F/190° C/Mark 5 for about 20 minutes Cover with foil and continue cooking for about 10 minutes
7. Serve with more walnuts or sliced banana on top.

Alison Watkins,
Weir Mill, Clifford,
Devon

BRANDY CREAMS

Serves 7

NO COOKING:

3 eggs, separated
2 tbs brandy
2 tbs honey
2 tbs lemon juice
2 tbs water
5 fl oz double cream

1. Blend egg yolks with all ingredients except whites and cream
2. Whisk whites and whip cream
3. Fold into mixture
4. Lightly oil 7 small ramekins and place mixture in them
5. Put ramekins in freezer
6. Serve with fan wafers.

Sheila Engelse,
New Malden,
Surrey

CHEESECAKE

6 oz shortcrust pastry or 4 sponge cakes
3 eggs
1½ lb curd cheese
5 oz double cream
7 oz caster sugar
2 oz flour
Pinch of salt
Grated rind and juice of 1 large lemon
8" loose-bottomed cake tin

1. Set oven at 350° F/Gas Mark 4
2. Grease bottom of tin with butter; flour bottom and sides
3. Crumble 4 sponge cakes evenly on bottom, or use shortcrust pastry as base
4. Mix cheese well with wooden spoon, then add flour and beat thoroughly
5. Add cream, salt, lemon juice and rind
6. Put eggs and sugar in another bowl and beat till light and creamy
7. Combine the two mixtures, again beating well Pour the result into prepared tin and bake on low shelf for approximately 1¼ hours.

Open oven door slightly, but leave cake for ¼ hour so that it does not relax too quickly.
Serve next day.

Steve Race,
"My Music" TV

CHOCOLATE CHEESE CAKE

8 oz chocolate digestive biscuits — crushed
4 oz melted butter
8 oz cream cheese
4 oz caster sugar
1 tsp vanilla essence
4 oz plain chocolate
2 eggs — separated
½ pint double cream
Crushed flake bar
8" cake tin

1. Mix crushed biscuits and butter and line tin
2. Beat cheese until smooth
   Stir in half sugar and all vanilla essence
3. Melt chocolate. When cool, slightly beat into cheese
   Add beaten egg yolks
4. Beat egg whites until stiff. Fold in remaining sugar
   Fold into chocolate mixture
5. Lightly whip cream and fold in
6. Turn into tin and refrigerate for 8 hours.

   To serve:
       Turn out and sprinkle crushed flake bar over.

   Will serve 8 people approx.
   2 tbs Brandy is a pleasant addition!

Sue Price,
Chagford, Devon

Dear Mrs Nyburg,
Thank you for your letter.
I really don't do this kind of thing you are after;
but put me down for any well-cooked chocolate
pudding if you like.

The Rt. Hon.
The Lord Home
of The Hirsel, K.T.

CHOCOLATE SPONGE PUDDING

4 oz butter or margarine
4 oz sugar
3 oz SR flour
2 large eggs, beaten
Pinch of salt
½ oz cocoa
½ oz cornflour
2 oz plain chocolate ⎫
1 tbs milk   ⎭ *melted together*

continued on next page

continued

1. Cream together butter and sugar
    Add eggs a little at a time
2. Mix cocoa, cornflour, salt and flour, sieve and fold
    into creamed mixture
3. Add melted chocolate and milk and stir
4. Grease 1½ pint pudding basin and put in mixture
    Cover with foil — Pleat foil in centre to allow for
    expansion during cooking
    Fasten foil with string
5. Stand basin in a saucepan with boiling water half
    way up sides of the basin
    Steam for 1½—2 hours.
    Chocolate Sauce:
    2 oz plain chocolate
    2 tbs water
    1 tsp cornflour
    ¾ gill milk
    1 tsp castor sugar
    ½ gill cream/evaporated milk
    ½ tsp vanilla essence

1. Melt chocolate with water, and boil until it becomes
    a smooth batter
2. Mix cornflour with milk, add to the chocolate with
    the sugar and stir until boiling
    Boil for 5 minutes
3. Add cream and vanilla when sauce has cooled a
    little
    Reheat carefully without boiling.

*This is a favourite recipe of mine — and I hope it
will please Lord Home of the Hirsel.*

Jean Nyburg

166

CHRISTMAS BREAD & BUTTER PUDDING

How to get rid of the Christmas pudding!

1. Butter a 1 pint pie dish
2. Fill with alternate layers of sliced bread and butter and sliced cold Christmas pudding
3. Heat 1 pint milk
   Add 2 tbs sugar and pour on to 2 beaten eggs
4. Stir well or whisk gently. Pour into a pie dish
5. Allow to soak into pudding mixture for 10 minutes
6. Bake in a moderate oven 375°F/200°C/Gas Mark 5 — about 30—40 minutes until set and slightly browned.

CAN BE EATEN HOT or COLD and is delicious with cream.

Dorothy L. Brown,
Bullers Arms,
Chagford

CINNAMON APPLE PUDDING

2 lb Bramleys
4 oz demerara sugar
4 oz brown breadcrumbs
  fairly coarse
2 full tsp cinnamon powder
2 oz white sugar
Good squeeze of lemon

1. Slice apples thinly into a deep ovenware dish
   Sprinkle on 2 oz white sugar and lemon juice
2. Mix brown sugar, breadcrumbs and cinnamon together, and cover apples with the mixture
3. Bake slowly for 30 minutes, then extra 5 or 10 minutes in high oven to be sure the top is crunchy
4. Serve very hot but not straight from the oven, to allow top to get crisp.

**Sir Peter Parker,
former Head of British Rail**

GOLDEN SPONGE PUDDING

Serves 4

A Philip Harben recipe

3 oz butter or margarine
6 oz SR flour
3 oz caster sugar
1 egg
Little golden syrup
Little milk

1. Grease 1¼ pt pudding basin
2. Put butter — which must not be hard from the fridge, or runny — into a mixing bowl with sugar Beat to a light cream
3. Work in beaten egg, little by little
4. Put a dollop of golden syrup in pudding basin and work it right round sides of basin with flat of a knife Do not stint syrup
5. Give mixture another quick beating, then fold in flour and work in enough milk for a dropping consistency
6. Scoop mixture into basin, cover and steam for at least 2 hours
7. Then turn lovely light pudding out on to a serving dish.

And as you lift off the basin
see the lovely molten syrup trickle down the sides
of the sponge to anoint it with golden glory!

Honor Blackman,
Famous actress

GOOSEBERRY & ALMOND SOUFFLÉ

8 oz fresh or frozen gooseberries
3 eggs, separated
4 tbs water
4 oz sugar (caster)
¾ tsp almond essence
1 sachet powdered gelatine
¼ pint double or whipping cream
To decorate, about 1 oz ratafias, crushed, and a little whipped cream.

1. Prepare 5" soufflé dish; overlap top by 2"−3" and oil paper
2. Wash or defrost gooseberries
   Cook gently 10 −15 minutes in a heavy pan until soft and broken up, stirring occasionally
   Rub through a sieve and measure ¼ pint purée
3. Whisk egg yolks and sugar over a pan of gently simmering water
   Remove from heat when thick and creamy and continue whisking until cool
4. Prepare gelatine and add to purée and almond essence. Fold into egg yolk mixture until evenly blended
5. Beat cream until it holds its shape, then fold into soufflé mixture
   Beat egg whites until stiff, then fold into the soufflé until evenly blended
   Pour into dish and chill 4 hours
6. Remove collar of dish, brush oil round edge of soufflé. Press crushed ratafias round edge
   Pipe a little whipped cream on centre
7. Serve chilled.

Rt Hon. Norman Tebbit MP

MUM'S BREAD PUDDINGS

½ lb stale bread
3 oz sugar
1 egg
2 oz butter
2 oz each of currants
            raisins
            sultanas
Pinch mixed spice and nutmeg
Grated rind of 1 lemon
Nearly ½ pint of milk

1. Soak the bread for half an hour in cold water
2. Squeeze it and mix with the fruit, sugar, lemon rind, melted fat and spices
3. Beat the egg and add this with enough milk to make a soft dropping mixture
4. Bake at Gas Mark 4 for about 2 hours.

Alec McCowen,
well-known stage & TV star

NANNY'S MIRACLE PUDDING

1 tbs butter/margarine
Nearly teacup of sugar
Nearly teacup of milk
2 tbs SR flour
2 eggs
Rind and juice of a lemon

1. Beat butter and sugar
2. Stir in flour and butter
3. Add yolks of eggs beaten in milk
4. Fold in beaten whites
5. Pour into greased dish
6. Bake 1¼ hours in slow oven, Gas Mark 1, with dish standing in water.

Alison Watkins,
Weir Mill,
Clifford, Devon

BERE REGIS

ORANGE FOOL

Serves 6

NO COOKING

1 stale cake
¾ pint double cream
Sugar to taste
2 lemons
4 oranges

1. Put sponge cake in bottom of glass dish
2. Mix together in a basin, grated rind of 1 lemon, 2 oranges and juice of all the fruit
3. Mix with cream and sugar
4. Pour over cake
5. Leave overnight in refrigerator.

Jean Nyburg

ORANGE GELÉE

Wanted:
> ¾ pint milk
> 2 new laid large eggs
> 1 packet gelatine
> 3/8th pint orange or lemon juice
> 4 oz granulated or caster sugar

Utensils:
> A large bowl; milk saucepan; scales; large plate; large knife; squeezer; cup for gelatine; boiling water; dessert spoon.

Method:
1. Separate eggs; yolks in bowl, whites on a plate. Whisk well. Squeeze out 3/8th pint fruit juice
   Cream yolks and sugar
2. Warm milk in saucepan and pour into bowl. Stir and return the contents of the bowl to the saucepan
   Over gentle heat, and stirring continually make the custard. It must *not* boil
   Put custard into the bowl
3. Prepare and add gelatine — stir it in. Add fruit juice Stir. Fold in whisked whites of eggs
4. Pour into a large glass bowl or into 6 individual bowls.

> Sidney F. Fooks M.C., M.A.
> Former English Master at
> Harrow County School
> for Boys 1922—1960

PARTY TREACLE TART

1. Line a pie dish with shortcrust pastry
2. Beat up 2 eggs and 3 tbs sugar
3. Melt 2 oz butter and 1 teacup of golden syrup
4. Beat into egg mixture
5. Add 1 tsp vanilla essence to chopped walnuts
6. Put into oven 275° –300° F for 1–1¼ hours.

Alison Watkins,
Weir Mill,
Clifford, Devon

PINEAPPLE CRUMB

6—7 digestive biscuits — finely rolled
6¼ oz double cream
4 rings pineapple
2 oz margarine
6—8 oz caster sugar
2 eggs

1. Sprinkle 1/3rd of the crumbs onto a greased tin with a loose base
2. Beat eggs, sugar and margarine as for a cake and spread on the crumbs
   Top with more crumbs
3. Beat cream until very stiff and add pineapple, chopped and well drained
4. Spread on top of crumbs in tin
5. Crumb again and put in fridge for at least 24 hours
6. Decorate if liked
7. Remove tin from base and put sweet onto a serving dish.

   This quantity fills a 7″ sandwich tin.

Josephine Binney R.I.B.A.
Sherborne, Dorset

176

STRAWBERRY HONEYCOMB MOULD

Serves 10—12

4 large eggs (separated)
2 oz caster sugar
2 pkts strawberry jelly
¼ pint double cream
3 pint jelly mould
2 pints milk

Mix egg yolks and sugar
until creamy, in a pan

Stir in milk and bring
custard to simmering point,
stirring all the time

Pour mixture into jelly mould

Leave to cool and refrigerate

Demould and decorate with
homemade brandy snaps
and lots of Devonshire cream!

Jean Nyburg

177

WATERMELON DESSERT

In summer, fill the centre
with a fresh fruit salad
Decorate with lots of whipped cream

In winter, fill the centre
with vanilla ice cream —
laced with whisky or
liqueur — and chocolate
sauce topped with slivers of
orange peel

Sue Daymond,
Catering Manageress of
Rank Xerox — London

Oh! Dear!

HOW TO MAKE CREAM

Take 8 pints of milk
Pour into a shallow, wide earthenware pan and
leave for 12 hours in warm weather or
24 hours in cold weather.

Turn gas to its lowest heat and place pan on
asbestos mat.

Heat very slowly and NEVER BOIL

When surface begins to ripple, and a solid
yellow rim appears, the pan can be carried into
the larder — hope your hand is steady!

Leave to cool for —
    12 hours in summer
    24 hours in winter

       Remove cream with a slotted spoon.

Oh! Dear!

AMBER PUDDING

July 1872

Line a pudding dish with puff pastry

Take: *½ lb fresh butter*
½ lb loaf sugar
8 eggs

Take the yolks of the eggs,
mix with the butter and
sugar on the fire, until it becomes
thick but not boiling.

Whip the whites of the eggs to a froth and mix
with the other when cold.

Add as much candied orange peel
beaten to a paste as will give colour and flavour.

Put marmalade or any kind of jam
at the bottom of the dish.

Pour the mixture over and bake for
half an hour.

From an old family Cookbook

Jane Niven,
Torhill, Devon

APRICOT BRULÉE

14 oz tin apricots, drained
2 drops almond essence
½ pint double cream — whipped stiffly
Soft brown sugar

1. Liquidise apricots. Add almond essence
2. Spread half cream in a shallow dish
   then pour in purée and cover with remaining cream
3. Chill 3—4 hours
4. Sprinkle sugar over top to depth of 1/8th"
5. Get grill blazing hot and grill sugar top
   until it caramelizes
6. Cool.

IT CAN BE FROZEN

Yvonne St. Claire Anderson,
Thornworthy,
Chagford

APRICOT CREAM CUSTARD

Custard:
1 pint milk
2 eggs
2 egg yolks
1½ tbs caster sugar

1. Scald milk (but do not let it boil)
2. Break eggs into a bowl and add extra yolks
3. Beat well with a fork but do not allow to get frothy
4. Add sugar and scalded milk
   Stir well
5. While milk is boiling, prepare a 2 pint soufflé dish
   Spread apricot jam over the bottom,
   pour on scalded milk mixture
6. Cover with foil and place in a
   roasting pan with water (or a bain marie) in a
   medium oven for about 45 minutes
7. When firm, remove from oven
   When cold place in refrigerator for 1 hour
8. Next, cover with another layer of jam and beat up
   8 oz of double cream and
   5 oz plain yoghurt. Mix together and cover custard
   and jam with the mixture
9. Sprinkle grated nutmeg generously over the cream.

Her Grace, the Duchess of Somerset,
Maiden Bradley, Wiltshire

ATHELBROSE

½ pint double cream
2 tbs honey
2 oz oatmeal
Whisky to taste

Toast oatmeal under grill
Whip double cream until
thick
Add oatmeal, honey and
whisky — Fold in.
Fresh fruit, such as
raspberries, and loganberries,
can also be added.

Rt. Hon. David Steel MP
Leader of the Liberal Party

BARBADOS CREAM

Serves 4

2 small cartons plain yoghurt
1 small carton double cream

1. Whip the cream and mix together with the
    yoghurt until smooth
2. Divide into small bowls or ramekins
    and top with a thick layer of soft brown sugar
3. Refrigerate for at least 2 hours before serving.

This recipe is also very good
made with apricot yoghurt
or
as above but with added ginger preserve or
chopped up preserved ginger and syrup.

Judi Dench,
One of our best known
and loved Stage & TV Stars

BREAD & BUTTER PUDDING

For five portions — that is to say, to suit a dinner party of eight at which three people are on a diet — make 6 generous butter sandwiches. Press together firmly, take off the rinds and cut each double slice into ½-inch cubes. Sprinkle half of these into a pie dish of a size for this amount of bread to occupy about a third. Now wash 3 oz of sultanas, heat them in a sherry-glass of sweet white vermouth and add half of these to the dish. Next take ½ lb of Tiptree's Little Scarlet strawberry jam, dilute with a coffee-cupful of boiling water and spoon half the resultant syrup evenly on to the dish. If you have followed these instructions as diligently as you ought, there will now be in your kitchen some more bread, alcoholic currants and liquid jam. With these make another layer.

In a pudding basin, well whisk 4 whole eggs, add 3 oz caster sugar and after a while pour in 1 pint of milk. Keep whisking until all is yellow and rich and slightly frothy . . . and then pour on to the top layer in the pie dish. Next, butter 3 slices of bread lightly on both sides, take off the rinds, square off and cut diagonally into quarters. These steam-baked isosceles triangles are then secured, long side down, in the soggy top of the pudding, so that the twelve protruding apexes make a handsome pattern. Now, or an hour before the dish is required, put it in the middle of a cool (mark 2/325° F) oven, and if the top triangles become brown rather than golden, lower the dish and paint the bread with a little melted butter.

Clement Freud MP

BROWN BREAD ICE CREAM

½ pint double cream
1 oz vanilla sugar
3 oz stale brown bread
3 oz soft dark brown sugar

1. Make the ice cream by whipping the cream and caster sugar lightly
2. Turn it into an ice tray or polythene container, cover and put in freezer — or freezer compartment of refrigerator at its lowest number
3. As mixture begins to harden round the edges, stir the sides into the middle
4. Make breadcrumbs from brown bread
   Spread them on an oiled baking tray and sprinkle with brown sugar
5. Put tray in oven 400° F/Mark 6 or under the grill until the sugar caramelizes with the bread
   Stir from time to time
6. When they are golden brown, leave them to cool and break them into crumbs again
7. When ice cream is semi-stiff, mix in the crumbs
8. Put container back in refrigerator freezing compartment for 2 more hours

AN ADULT REFINEMENT: Pour a little brandy over each portion before serving!

Mary Every,
Furlong, Chagford

CHOCOLATE FUDGE PUDDING

4 oz SR flour
4 oz sugar
2 oz melted butter
{ 4 oz soft brown sugar
{ 2 oz cocoa
1 tsp vanilla essence
Pinch of salt
½ teacup milk
2 oz cocoa

1. Mix all ingredients — except the cocoa and
   soft brown sugar — and put in fireproof dish
2. Top with brown sugar and cocoa mixed together —
   and pour 1 teacup of hot water over the lot
3. Bake at Gas Mark 4/350° F for 50 minutes.

*Comes out miraculously every time
with its own chocolate sauce.*

*GORGEOUSLY SINFUL WITH
CLOTTED CREAM!!*

Liz Arden,
Chagford,
Devon

CRÊME BRULÉE

2½ pints single cream
12 egg yolks
2 level tbs caster sugar
1 tsp vanilla essence
4 level tbs demerara sugar

1. Put cream in top half of a double boiler, or in a bowl over a pan of simmering water
2. Carefully stir in the egg yolks beaten with the caster sugar and vanilla essence into the warm cream
3. Continue cooking gently until the cream has thickened enough to coat the back of a wooden spoon
4. Strain cream through a fine sieve into a soufflé dish and leave to chill for at least 4 hours, or overnight.

"Then I make a toffee with sugar and water in a double saucepan until it becomes nice and brown and then pour it over the cold dish the next day.

Serve — It's delicious!"

Christopher Biggins,
TV and Stage star

EGGS à la NEIGE

3 egg whites
3 cups milk
2 tbs sugar
1 package vanilla pudding mix

1. Beat egg white until foamy, add
   sugar and beat until stiff but not dry
2. Scald the milk
3. Drop egg white meringue by teaspoonfuls into
   the hot milk. Cover and let stand for 3 minutes
4. Remove meringues carefully and put them on a
   towel to drain and cool
5. Combine pudding mix and the milk in which
   meringues were cooked and cook until mixture
   boils, stirring constantly
6. Remove from heat, cool for 10 minutes
   stirring once
7. Pour pudding into a shallow serving bowl
   Top with meringues.

SERVE WARM OR CHILLED

**Liza Minelli,
International Stage
and Film Star**

FRENCH PANCAKES

1860

Beat up in basins the whites
and yolks of 5 eggs separately

Mix the yolks with 2 oz flour,
the rind of a lemon — grated,
¾ pint of cream and
1 oz sifted sugar.

Then mix the whites of the eggs stiff —
having buttered 8 saucers.

Put the same quantity into
each and bake them 20 minutes.

When baked, lay a little
preserved peel on each and
a sift of sugar over the top.

Sheelagh Knox,
from an old family cookbook,
belonging to the Knox family

191

FRESH PEACH CRUMBLE

½ oz butter
6 peaches, poached in
4 oz sugar and 4 tbs water
Crumble:
4 oz flour
3 oz butter
2 oz brown sugar

PREHEAT OVEN to Gas Mark 4/350° F/180° C

1. Lightly grease medium sized baking dish with butter
2. Arrange sliced peaches in dish and cover with remaining syrup
3. Make crumble by mixing butter and flour to breadcrumb consistency and then stir in brown sugar
4. Cover fruit with crumble mixture
5. Bake for 45 minutes.

Serve at once with cream

Christopher Dean,
Skating Partner of Jayne Torvill
World Champion Skaters
from Nottingham

GINGER MOUSSE

4 eggs
2 tbs water
1 oz gelatine
4 oz caster sugar
5 or 6 pieces preserved ginger
4 tbs golden syrup
¼ pint whipped cream

1. Separate eggs and melt gelatine in hot water until dissolved
2. Beat 4 egg yolks with the sugar until light and creamy
3. Add dissolved gelatine and ¼ pint of whipped cream and the ginger syrup Mix well together
4. Whip 4 egg whites until stiff and fold into mixture
5. Finally add the ginger, chopped into small pieces
6. Pour into a wet soufflé dish and decorate with slices of ginger.

CHILL in refrigerator until needed
or can be deep frozen.

Dame Nancy Snagge D.B.E.
Director of W.R.A.F. 1950–56
ADC to HM the Queen

GINGER PINEAPPLE CREAM

Line the bottoms of
individual dishes with
crushed ginger biscuits
Moisten with sherry or with
pineapple juice.

Cover with crushed — or slices of —
pineapple and then whipped
double cream.

Decorate
with pineapple and crushed
ginger biscuits.

Serve Chilled

Mrs Judith Cosford,
Chagford,
Devon

JAYNE'S TRIFLE

1 pkt sponge cakes
1 raspberry jelly
Fresh raspberries
2 oz sugar
1 pint custard
¼ lb double cream

1. Make raspberry jelly
2. Line a bowl with sponge cakes
   Cover with raspberries
3. Sprinkle sugar over fruit
4. Pour jelly on, and leave to set
5. Cover with 1 pint custard and
   whipped double cream
6. Decorate with a few raspberries.

WARNING
DO NOT SKATE IMMEDIATELY
AFTERWARDS —
it is rather filling!

Jayne Torvill,
World famous Skater,
Partner of Christopher Dean,
Nottingham

LEICESTER CREAMS

December 1850

*An ancient recipe from an old
family cookery book belonging
to the Niven family.*

Take the juice of a good-sized lemon and a half —
the peel having been rubbed with
lumps of sugar to get the flavour

Add to 3 or 4 oz refined sugar
and 1½ gills of raisin wine

Pour into a pint of good cream
stirring gently

Beat together *one way* for
a quarter of an hour, and pour
into glasses.

Jane Niven,
Torhill,
Devon

PARTY BAKED CUSTARD

1. Scald 1 pint of milk — let it cool
2. Beat 3 large eggs, sweeten to taste
   and make a baked custard in a soufflé dish
3. When cold, spread with raspberry jam
   Cover with crushed ratafia and
   top with whipped cream, sweetened and
   flavoured with vanilla.

   Variations:
1. Coffee-flavoured baked custard
   spread with puréed apricots, then ratafia, and
   the whipped cream

2. Coffee-flavoured custard, topped with a
   drained compôte of cape gooseberries
   (cape goldenberries).
   Serve cream separately.

   An old Irish family favourite

Rhoda Lewis,
Chagford,
Devon

PAVLOVA

4 egg whites
½ tsp vanilla essence
1 tsp cornflour
½ lb fruit
8 oz caster sugar
*1 tsp vinegar (***not*** malt)*
½ pint double cream

1. Draw 8" circle on non-stick paper
   Place on baking sheet
2. Whisk egg whites until stiff, beat in
   sugar, 1 tbs at a time
3. Beat in vanilla essence, vinegar and cornflour
4. Spoon meringue mixture over the round,
   making a slight hollow in the centre
5. Cook in a slow oven for about 1 hour until firm
6. Leave to cool, then remove paper
   Place on a serving plate
7. Lightly whip cream and pile in hollow
8. Top with strawberries or any fruit in season.

Maggie Ryder,
**Leading actress — starring
in the West End**

RUM TRUFFLE for CHRISTMAS

3 oz plain chocolate
1 egg yolk
½ oz butter
1 tsp rum
1 tsp single cream

1. Melt chocolate in a small bowl over hot
   (not boiling water)
2. Add one egg yolk, butter, rum and cream
3. Beat mixture until thick
4. Then chill in refrigerator until
   firm enough to handle
5. Shape mixture into 12 balls and roll in
   chocolate vermicelli or drinking chocolate.

Anne Nevill
Y.T.S. Catering Training Office,
London

SPECIAL LEMON SPONGE PUDDING

1 pkt trifle sponges
4 oz butter
2 large eggs
2 small lemons
5 oz sugar
¼ pint double cream

1. Grease a 1 lb loaf tin and line with slices of sponge
2. Beat butter and sugar until light, add egg yolks, lemon juice and grated rind
   (It will curdle — but do not PANIC!)
3. Whisk whites until stiff and fold into the mixture
4. Put a layer of the mixture into the tin with more slices of sponge on top — repeat
5. Cover firmly with cling film and refrigerate until required
6. Turn on to a dish
7. Whip the cream until stiff and cover the pudding Decorate with orange and lemon slices.

This sweet freezes very well and improves with being made a day in advance as the lemon juice is absorbed by the sponge.
DELICIOUS!

Mary Hasler,
Chagford

TARTE à l'ORANGE

10 oz sifted plain flour
1 oz ground almonds
½ oz best unsalted butter
2 egg yolks
1 tsp salt

Filling:
4 thin skinned and very ripe oranges
plus their weight in sugar.

1. Make pastry. This is very rich and is best chilled a little before rolling
2. Put oranges, sugar and enough water to cover in a large pan. Boil until quite soft
3. Remove from pan. Liquidise and sieve
4. Roll out pastry to fit a buttered and floured loose bottomed 10" flan tin
5. Bake at 400°F or Gas Mark 6 for 12—15 minutes
6. Cool, then fill with orange purée and bake again, just enough to glaze the oranges.

SERVE HOT with WHIPPED CREAM!

HRH the Duchess of Kent,
Patron of Cancer Relief

WORK, REST and PLAY PUDDING

This quantity is for
1 serving
Just increase as required.

1 scoop ice cream
1 Mars bar
1 tbs double cream
1 measure brandy
1 tsp water

1. Melt Mars bar in water in bowl over heat until thoroughly gooey!
2. Stir in cream
3. Stir in brandy
4. Pour mixture over ice cream and serve.

The resultant taste varies according to the amount of brandy used.

A delicious, frighteningly fattening confection!!

Molly Russell,
Cannock, Staffs

202

Cakes and Bread

AMERICAN BROWNIES

"These succulent, chocolatey delights — which I discovered in the "wilds" of Michigan — are like naughty Banbury cakes, and hence can prove extremely fattening — but then there is always moderation!"

2 oz plain chocolate
2 eggs, beaten
2 oz plain flour
1 tsp baking powder
4 oz butter
8 oz granulated sugar
4 oz chopped hazelnuts
¼ tsp salt

1. Preheat oven to 350° F/180° C/Gas Mark 4 and line base of well greased oblong tin 7" x 11" with greaseproof paper
2. Place butter and broken up chocolate in top of double saucepan
When they have melted stir in rest of ingredients
3. Spread this mixture all over the lined tin and bake 30 minutes or until you can take a knife cleanly through the mixture
4. Leave in tin to cool for about 10 minutes — then cut into 15 squares and put them on a wire rack to finish cooling.

Julian Lloyd Webber,
World famous Cellist

AUNTY HILARY'S CHOCOLATE CAKE

This makes 3 x 7" sandwich tins

4 medium eggs
½ lb margarine
1 tbs coffee
½ lb caster sugar
2 oz cornflour
2 oz cocoa powder
4 oz SR flour

1. Cream fat and sugar till very pale and fluffy
2. Mix all dry ingredients together
3. Add eggs one by one —
   adding a little flour with each egg
   (Do this at lowest speed if using a mixer)
4. Put in greaseproof-lined tins
   Cook at Mark 4 for ½ hour
5. Ice with coffee butter icing.

Hilary Turnbull,
Cowbridge, Cardiff

BANANA BISCUITS

2 dried bananas
6 tbs orange juice
6 oz wholewheat flour
2 oz medium oatmeal
4 tbs corn oil
1 beaten egg

1. Heat oven to 350° F/180° C/Gas Mark 4
2. Finely chop bananas and put into saucepan with orange juice
3. Bring to the boil and simmer for 10 minutes or until soft
4. Liquidise
5. Mix flour and oatmeal in bowl, pour in oil, egg and banana mixture and mix to a smooth dough
6. Roll out 1/8th" thick — cut into 1½" to 2" rounds
7. Bake for 20 minutes.

Throwleigh W.I.

BROWN BREAD

1 large and 1 small loaf

¾ pint warm water
12 oz strong plain flour
12 oz wholemeal flour
1 tsp sugar
2 tsp salt
1 oz fresh yeast
small handful of bran
1 tbs wheat germ
1 dsp vegetable oil

1. Preferably with a Kenwood Chef and a dough hook into a largish bowl, put water and yeast and mix by hand till yeast has dissolved
2. Add oil and mix by hand again
3. Measure flour, salt, sugar, bran, wheatgerm and tip into bowl with yeast mixture
4. With dough hook — or hand — mix all together till dough comes clean away from sides of bowl
5. On a floured bowl turn out the dough and push it around for a few more seconds
   There will be enough for 1 large and 1 small tin
6. With a sharp knife, cut off 1/3rd dough for the small tin. Grease tins with lard, including corners
   Mould dough, put in tins and cover with towel
   Leave in warm place
7. Set oven to Mark 6 and leave till dough rises to top of tins — 25—35 minutes
8. Put in centre of oven 30—40 minutes
   Cool on a wire tray

Rt. Rev David Sheppard,
Bishop of Liverpool

CHAGFORD FRUIT LOAF

8 fl oz cold tea
6 oz granulated sugar
6—8 oz mixed fruit
10 oz SR flour
2 oz butter or margarine
1 large egg

1. Melt tea, sugar, fruit and fat and simmer 2—3 mins
2. Cool until lukewarm and add
   beaten egg and sieved flour
3. Mix well and pour into a 2 lb loaf tin, well greased
   and lined on the bottom
4. Bake at 350° F/180°C/Mark 4
   for 1—1¼ hours.

Mrs Frances Kenna,
Chagford

CHALLAH

3 lbs plain fine flour
3 oz fresh yeast
3 tbs salt
1 glass sugar
1½ glasses oil
2 glasses warm water
1 egg

PREHEAT OVEN TO 425° F

1. Put 3 lb flour in bowl
   Make well in centre, add sugar and yeast
2. Place salt around border, add oil and warm water
3. Mix together, then allow to stand near warm oven for 15 minutes
4. Knead until smooth dough texture adding more flour if the mixture is sticky
5. Allow to stand, covered, near warm oven until risen — about 25 minutes
6. Take CHALLAH (small piece of dough) make appropriate BRACHA and burn this, then throw it away
7. Form shape of loaf and lay on greased tin
   Brush with egg
   Stand further 5—10 minutes
8. Bake approx 25—30 minutes until firm underneath

The Chief Rabbi and
Lady Jakobovits

CHERRY CAKE

8 oz SR flour
4 oz margarine
4 oz caster sugar
4 oz cherries (halved)
¼ tsp salt
2 eggs
1 tbs milk

1. Cream fat and sugar together
2. Beat in eggs one at a time
3. Sieve flour and salt into mixture
4. Add milk, and lastly the cherries —
   coated with flour to stop them sinking
5. Put in prepared tin and bake in a moderate oven
   for about 1 hour or until firm to touch

Margery Preston

CHOCOLATE TOFFEE FINGERS

*Even thinking about these puts
on weight!*

2 oz syrup
4 oz sugar
6 oz plain flour
8 oz margarine
2 oz caster sugar
4 oz cooking chocolate
1 small can condensed milk

1. Cream 4 oz margarine with 2 oz caster sugar
2. Sieve flour and fold in
3. Press into greased tin 10" x 8" and prick
4. Bake at 375° for approximately 20 minutes.

Topping:
1. Heat 4 oz margarine; 4 oz sugar; 2 oz syrup and condensed milk in pan over low heat until sugar is dissolved and mixture starts to boil
2. Continue boiling for 10—15 minutes, stirring until toffee is thick and golden
3. Pour it over the cooled shortbread base and leave to set
4. Melt cooking chocolate and pour over set toffee
5. Leave to cool and cut . . .
   then eat!!!

Pam Johnston,
Chagford,
Devon

CHOCOLATE VICTORIA SANDWICH

4 oz margarine
5 oz caster sugar
3 oz SR flour
1 oz cocoa
1 tsp baking powder
1 tbs hot water
2 eggs
Vanilla essence

1. Cream margarine, sugar and beat in eggs
2. Add hot water. Sift in dry ingredients
3. Grease and flour 2 sandwich tins
4. Bake cakes in moderate oven for approximately 10 minutes
5. When cool, finish with a chocolate butter icing filling and glacé icing top.

Sheelagh Knox,
Well Farm,
Throwleigh,
Devon

COURGETTE BREAD

American

2 medium courgettes
2 cups plain flour
¾ tsp each salt and bicarbonate soda
½ tsp baking powder
1 cup sugar
½ cup vegetable oil
2 eggs
½ cup walnuts
1½ tsp vanilla or 2 tbs sherry
1½ tsp cinnamon or
   1 tsp grated lemon zest and
   ½ tsp nutmeg

1. Grease ends of 5" x 9" loaf pan well
2. Line sides and bottom with greaseproof paper
3. Scrub courgettes but do not peel
4. Shred courgettes
5. Combine flour, salt, soda, baking powder, cinnamon and sugar
6. Add eggs, oil, vinegar and walnuts
7. Add shredded courgettes
8. Pour into prepared pan
9. Bake in 325° F oven for 1¼ hours
   or until bread shrinks slightly from sides of pan.

TIP: *Always keep some lemon and orange rind in the freezer. It grates very easily when frozen!*

Anne Seery,
Boulder, Colorado, USA

213

DATE and WALNUT BREAD

Canadian

2¾ oz cups sifted plain flour
4 tsp baking powder
¾ cup chopped walnuts
1½ cups milk
1 tsp salt
¾ cup brown sugar
1 cup cut-up dates
3 tbs salad oil

1. Sift flour, salt and baking powder into bowl
2. Add brown sugar, nuts and dates
3. Beat egg, milk and salad oil together lightly with a fork. Add to dry ingredients
4. Pour into a greased 9" x 5" x 3" loaf tin
   Stand for 20 minutes
5. Heat oven to 350° F
   Bake for 60—70 minutes until skewer inserted in centre comes out clean
6. Put on wire rack to cool.

Eileen Renny,
Canada

214

GINGERBREAD

12 oz plain flour
1 tsp baking powder
1 tsp bicarb
¼ tsp salt
1 tsp ginger powder

1. Sieve above ingredients together in a mixing bowl
2. Over a low heat in saucepan, melt and warm:-

   6 oz margarine
   6 oz soft brown sugar
   4 oz black treacle
   4 oz golden syrup

3. Stir frequently till sugar is melted
   DO NOT BOIL

4. Beat two eggs with 1/3rd pint warm milk
5. Beat all liquids into flour mixture
6. Pour into greased and lined tin 11" x 9"
7. Bake for 1½ hours at 325°F/165°C/Gas Mark 3
8. When cold, cut through middle and spread
   generously with butter icing
   Sandwich together.

Mrs Dorothy L. Brown,
Bullers Arms,
Chagford

GINGER SPONGE with MARMALADE

2 eggs
4 oz butter
2 oz soft brown sugar
2 tbs warm golden syrup
4 oz SR flour
¼ tsp baking powder
½ tsp ground ginger
Marmalade

1. Cream butter, sugar and syrup
2. When light and fluffy, work in beaten eggs
3. Fold in flour sifted with baking powder and ginger
4. Place in 2 greased 7 inch tins
   Bake at 400° F for 25 minutes
5. Turn out on a wire rack and cool
6. Sandwich together liberally with marmalade, and sprinkle with icing sugar.

Throwleigh W.I.
Devon

HELLO DOLLIES!

3 oz butter
6 oz chocolate chips
3 oz chopped walnuts
1 x 14 oz can condensed milk
3 oz digestive biscuit crumbs
3 oz sweetened dessicated coconut

8" x 8" baking tin

1. Add digestive biscuit crumbs to melted butter
2. Put in bottom of tin
3. Sprinkle with chocolate chips
4. Add coconut and spread evenly
5. Pour condensed milk over mixture
   and press nuts evenly into mixture
6. Bake at 350°F for 30 minutes
7. Allow to cool before cutting into squares.

WARNING: *LOCK UP THE CAKE TIN!!*

Anne Seery,
Boulder, Colorado, USA

LITTLE JOHN'S CAKES

June 1862

A recipe from an old family cookery book
belonging to the Knox family of Throwleigh.

Beat 6 ounces of butter to a cream
    Add 3 eggs well beaten, with the whites
    6 oz of sugar, finely ground
    ¼ lb currants, washed and dried
    1 lb of fine flour
Beat all for some time. Then dredge
flour on tin plates and drop the
mixture in small rounds.
Bake in a brisk oven.

Sheelagh Knox,
Well Farm,
Throwleigh,
Devon

218

MALT LOAF

10 oz SR flour
4 oz dried fruit
2 oz margarine
3 tbs golden syrup
Just over ¼ pint milk
Pinch of salt
¼ tsp bicarb
2 oz sugar
2 tbs ovaltine

1. Melt margarine, sugar and syrup in saucepan
2. Stir in milk and ovaltine
   but *DO NOT BOIL*
3. Put dry ingredients in mixing bowl, stir in
   liquid and mix thoroughly
4. Put in 2 small or 1 large loaf tin
5. Bake in moderate oven for about 1 hour.

Molly Russell,
Cannock, Staffs

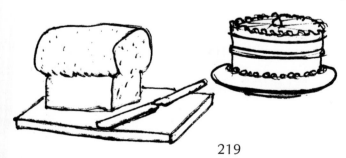

ORANGE and WALNUT CAKE

8 oz SR flour
6 oz butter
3 large eggs
1 oz chopped mixed peel
½ tsp salt
6 oz sugar
Rind of 1 large orange
2 oz walnuts
1 tbs concentrated orange juice

1. Sift flour and salt together
2. Cream butter and sugar
3. Add beaten eggs
4. Add half flour and the other ingredients and blend
5. Add remaining flour
6. Spoon mixture into a greased 7" cake tin
7. Cook in a moderate oven for 1¼ hours
   Icing:
   8 oz icing sugar
   2–3 tbs concentrated orange juice
1. Warm icing sugar and orange juice
   in a pan until smooth
2. Ice the cake while icing is still warm.
   BE CAREFUL not to OVERHEAT ICING
   when blending

Rt. Hon. Margaret Thatcher MP,
Prime Minister

ORANGE CHOCOLATE DRIZZLE CAKE

6 oz luxury margarine
6 oz caster sugar
3 eggs
2 tbs cold milk
Finely grated rind of 2 oranges
Orange Syrup:
Juice of 2 small oranges
4 oz sugar
> Boil together until sugar
> has dissolved

Chocolate Topping:
4 oz plain chocolate
½ oz butter
> Heat together in bowl over
> gently simmering water

1. Grease 2 lb loaf tin and line with greaseproof paper
2. Cream margarine and sugar
3. Beat in eggs, one at a time
4. Fold in sifted flour and add milk
   with last tbs of flour. Add orange rind
5. Turn mixture into tin and bake
   at 350° F for 1 hour
6. Turn on to wire rack and allow to cool
7. When almost cold make slits across top of cake
   with sharp knife
   Then "drizzle" prepared syrup across top,
   so that it soaks into cake
   Spread chocolate topping in whirls over top of cake.

Pauline Truscott,
Chagford, Devon

PINEAPPLE CAKE

3 rings of pineapple
4 oz caster sugar
8 oz SR flour
2 eggs
4 tbs milk
4 oz margarine
For Topping:
2 tbs icing sugar
1—2 tsp pineapple juice

1. Grease and line 6" cake tin
2. Chop 2½ pineapple rings into small pieces
3. Whisk eggs and milk together
4. Beat sugar and margarine — add chopped pineapple
5. Stir in flour, then egg mixture
6. Pour into tin. Cook at Mark 4 for 1¼—1½ hours
7. Decorate top with remaining ½ slice of pineapple — cut
8. Mix topping and pour over cake while hot.

Allow cake to cool before removing
from tin.

Throwleigh W.I.
Devon

222

REAL CHOCOLATE ICING

To ice two 7—8 inch layers

3 tbs water
½ lb plain chocolate
2 egg yolks

1. Measure water into saucepan and bring to boil
2. Draw off heat and add chocolate in pieces
3. Stir until melted
4. Blend in egg yolks
5. Beat after each egg is added.

   It will go shiny and thicken
   While still warm, spoon on cake
   It will set firm, but not too hard
   to cut.

Millicent Davies,
Chagford,
Devon

SHILSTONE MUSIC CAKE

A strange name — but to those of us who are lucky enough to live in Chagford, it is quite explicit.

Shilstone is a house mentioned in the Domesday Book. At regular intervals, there are concerts in the house, and at supper there is wine and cheese and cake and apple pie. Here is the cake recipe —

8 oz currants
8 oz stoned raisins
2 oz glaće cherries (cut)
8 oz sultanas
2 oz mixed peel
2 tbs milk
1 level tsp baking powder
6 oz margarine
6 oz sugar
5 eggs

1. Prepare an 8-inch cake tin by lining with greaseproof paper
2. Place all ingredients in a mixer or large bowl
    Mix well
3. Place in prepared tin
4. Bake in middle shelf of oven Gas Mark 3/ 315°F for 3—4 hours. Test with a knitting needle
5. Remove from oven and leave for 10 minutes
    Turn on to rack.
        Can be eaten the same day

Cake can be made with 1 lb mixed fruit and orange and lemon peel added. Blanched almonds can be put on top.

Jill Jory,
Shilstone,
Chagford

SUGARY BALLS

Ideal wet weather occupation
even for very small children!

2 oz sugar
6 oz SR flour
4 oz butter or margarine
Extra sugar
1 level tbs cocoa powder (optional)

1. Mix all ingredients together beyond
   breadcrumb stage until it is all a lovely doughy ball
2. Break off small walnut sized bits and roll in ball of
   hand into a round
3. Roll in extra sugar and put on a baking tray
4. Leave plenty of room between balls and bake in
   moderate oven for 30—50 minutes,
   depending on heat of oven
   They should rise slightly and split a little bit
5. Cool on a wire rack.

Marcia Gay,
Chagford,
Devon

TEN O'CLOCKS and FOUR O'CLOCKS

Canadian

Oatmeal Cookies

"My Grandfather never had elevenses —
just ten o'clocks and
four o'clocks!"

2 cups plain flour
2 cups porridge oats
1 cup brown sugar
1 cup butter
1 tsp soda dissolved in ¼ cup of hot water
½ tsp salt
Dash of nutmeg
¼ tsp vanilla

1. Mix in order
2. Roll in balls
3. Place on baking sheet and press down with base of a glass dipped each time in sugar
   (Rub base with butter to keep from sticking)
4. Using tines of fork — "cross hatch" and bake in moderate oven for 10 minutes at 375°
5. Cool on rack.

YIELD: 60 COOKIES

N.B. *1 cup equals 8 fl oz in English!*

Mary Rankin,
Gidleigh,
Devon

TONY'S GRANARY BREAD

2 tsps dried yeast
1 lump of sugar
1 teacup warm water

1. Stir up — and leave to rise
2. **Take:**
   3 lb granary flour
   1 lb strong white flour
   2 oz butter
   1 pint milk

Stir up together. Put in yeast mixture —
and put to rise for 1 hour

Have a bath and breakfast, then:

3. Knock it back and roll it into loaf size lumps
4. Shape
5. Cook for 35 minutes at high speed
6. Take out and cool and eat — dripping with lots of
   butter and homemade lemon cheese.

HEALTH WARNING: Waistlines vanish at once

Can be made in loaf size batches and frozen.

Tony Warner,
Wormshill,
Kent

WALNUT CRISPS

4 oz SR flour
4 oz soft brown sugar
1½ oz butter or margarine
1 oz walnuts
2 oz plain chocolate
1 small egg

1. Rub fat into flour
2. Add chopped walnuts
   brown sugar, the chocolate
   grated on coarse grater,
   and the egg. Mix well
3. Place in small heaps on a
   greased baking tray, allowing room to spread
4. Cook in a moderate oven for 15 minutes
5. Leave to cool slightly
   before putting on a cooling tray.

Throwleigh W.I.
Devon

WELSH CAKES

Makes 18 cakes

> 1 lb SR flour
> 4 oz sugar
> 1 egg
> ½ lb butter or margarine
> ½ lb currants
> Pinch of salt
> 10—12 fl oz milk

1. Cut fat into small pieces, rub in flour,
   salt and sugar with fingertips
   until like fine breadcrumbs
2. Stir in currants; beat together egg and milk
   and pour on to dry ingredients
3. Mix with a knife until mixture begins
   to bind together into a ball
4. Turn on to lightly floured board
   and knead gently until free from cracks
5. Roll out ¼" thick and cut into 3" rounds
6. Rub griddle with lard and warm over moderate heat
   Transfer cut mixture on to griddle and cook until
   brown on underside — then turn and leave for
   about 5—7 minutes until cooked.

SERVE HOT with butter

*Sir Harry would like to point out the he can no longer
eat these delicacies because he is diabetic, and he has
to watch his weight, too. Very sad, because they are
so good!*

**Sir Harry Secombe,
Everybody's favourite star**

"WET NELLIES" or LORD NELSON CAKE

Old Liverpool
Lamp Standard

Use as either a cake or a pudding.
A traditional Liverpool recipe.

8 oz shortcrust pastry
8 oz stale cake crumbs
4 oz raisins
4 tbs milk
4 oz golden syrup
Grated rind and juice of 1 lemon
Sprinkle of demerara sugar

1. Line a 7" sandwich tin with pastry
2. Mix cake crumbs with raisins, lemon rind and juice, syrup and milk
3. Put in pastry case and cover with rest of pastry Seal edges
4. Brush with milk and sprinkle with brown sugar
5. Bake at Gas Mark 5/375°F for 35 minutes.

P. Richardson,
Blundellsands,
Liverpool

What's for Dinner?

*A good dinner sharpens the wit
and softens the heart*

MY FAVOURITE MEAL

I don't know about a recipe — I usually just eat the finished product, leaving the ingredients to the cook responsible.

However, I give you below my favourite meal, which as you see, leaves very little to the imagination!

Prawn Cocktail

Roast Beef & Yorkshire Pudding

Potatoes & Vegetables

Lancashire Cheese & Biscuits.

**Billy Beaumont O.B.E.
our much loved former
English Rugby Captain**

And what an appropriate meal!

SOME PEBBLE MILL DINNER RECIPES

TERRINE DE LEGUME *(Vegetable Terrine)*

Ingredients (for 10 people)

CHICKEN FORCEMEAT

160 g (7 oz) White chicken meat (without skin)
40 cl (12 oz) Double cream
75 g (3 oz) Watercress with stalks removed
Salt and freshly ground pepper

1. Remove the sinew from the meat and mince finely
2. Put in a bowl on ice and allow to cool well
3. Mix in the cream a little at a time until a light airy mixture is formed
4. Liquidise the watercress with a little chicken stock
5. Mix a third of the farce with the watercress purée
6. Season both farces with salt and pepper

Note: *Steps 1 and 3 can be done in a blender as long as the chicken and cream are well chilled beforehand.*

continued on next page

VEGETABLES

40 g (1½ oz) Mange-tout, stringed & blanched
10 seconds
80 g (3¼ oz) Green beans, stringed & blanched
quickly
350 g (12 oz) Small carrots, peeled, blanched and
cut into quarters or sticks lengthwise
400 g (14 oz) Broccoli, cleaned & blanched quickly
200 g (7 oz) Small courgettes, blanched & cut
into quarters lengthwise
100 g (4 oz) Small mushrooms, cleaned &
blanched
10 g (½ oz) Butter
Salt & freshly ground pepper
Tomatoes cut into quarters &
watercress to garnish

1. Butter a terrine dish and spread the bottom with the chicken and watercress purée farce
2. Bed the carrot sticks (or quarters) well into this mixture. Season
3. Place a thin layer of the white chicken farce on top of the carrots so that they are just covered
4. Continue with another layer of vegetable then farce until the dish is full, seasoning each layer
5. Cover and poach in a bain-marie in a moderate oven for 35—40 minutes
6. Turn out when cool and arrange in individual slices on a tomato vinaigrette and garnish with tomato quarters and watercress.

TOMATO VINAIGRETTE

20 cl (6 fl oz) Chicken stock
20 g (¾ oz) Tomato purée
100 g (4 oz) Ripe tomatoes
5 cl (2 fl oz) Red wine vinegar
5 cl (2 fl oz) Olive oil
Salt & freshly ground pepper
and a little sugar & lemon juice

1. Mix the chicken stock with the tomato purée
2. Liquidise the fresh tomatoes and add to the above mixture with the vinegar
3. Add the olive oil very slowly and season — if necessary add sugar and lemon juice to taste.

STEAK AU POIVRE A LA PEBBLE MILL

(Ingredients for two people)

500 g (18 oz) Fillet steak, well trimmed &
seasoned with salt
½ tbs each of Black & white peppercorns
½ tbs Green peppercorns
1½ fl oz Olive oil
1½ fl oz Cognac
1½ fl oz Madeira
1½ fl oz Fresh cream

1. In the centre of a folded tea towel, crush the black and white peppercorns coarsley with a mallet
2. Lay the steak on the black and white peppercorns, pressing gently all round so the pepper clings to the sides
3. Heat the olive oil in a frying pan and cook quickly over high heat turning two or three times
4. Remove the steak on to a hot plate and keep in a warm place
5. Pour the cognac into the original pan and set light to it. Reduce the heat
6. When the flame has died away, add first the Madeira, then the cream, stirring continuously over a low heat until the sauce thickens
7. Add the green peppercorns
8. Arrange steak on hot plates and spoon the sauce onto the steaks.

TEUILLE AMANDES MARJORIE

(Ingredients for 4 people)

TEUILLE PASTE

6 Egg whites
225 g (8 oz) Plain flour
225 g (8 oz) Icing sugar
150 g (5½ oz) Unsalted butter (melted)

1. Place the egg whites, plain flour and icing sugar in blender and blend well
2. Add melted butter and blend again
3. Pour paste into a container and set aside

To make the Teuilles:

1. Trim the rim off the lid of a plastic ice cream container
2. Make a template by cutting out a circle or a rectangle to the size required from the centre
3. Set oven to Gas Mark 5/190C/375F
4. Place the template on a lightly buttered non-stick baking tray and with a palette knife, spread the teuille paste, covering the circle or rectangle
5. Lift off the template and your shape should be formed
6. Cover the paste with chopped almonds as desired
   These teuilles will be used for the base of the sweet
7. On another baking tray follow the same method as above, omitting the chopped almonds
8. Place both the trays in the oven for 8—10 min until lightly browned
   Remove
9. Carefully with a thin knife, slide under teuilles and lift off
   Keep in a warm place.

continued on next page

To finish:

> *2 Peaches, peeled, halved & sliced horizontally*
> *(apples or pears may be used)*
> *4 dsp of brown sugar*
> *150 ml (5 fl oz) Raspberry syrup*
> *150 ml (5 fl oz) Apricot syrup*
> *150 ml (5 fl oz) Whipped cream*
> *Icing sugar*

1. Place the peaches on a good strong wooden chopping board
2. Cover each with the brown sugar
3. With a very hot iron of some description (Granny's flat iron perhaps)
   lightly touch the brown sugar and burn a glaze
4. Place the teuilles with almonds on plates
5. On them place the caramelized peaches
6. Pipe cream over the top of the peach
7. Place the plain teuilles on top dusted with icing sugar
8. Carefully pour the raspberry and apricot syrup around the plate to form a nice pattern
   Serve.

RASPBERRY & APRICOT SYRUPS

600 ml (1 pint) Water
500 g (18 oz) Caster sugar
Juice of 1½ lemons
250 g (9 oz) Raspberries — fresh or tinned
250 g (9 oz) Apricots — fresh or tinned

1. In a stainless steel saucepan, gently bring the water and caster sugar to the boil and gently simmer for 20 minutes
2. Set the syrup aside to cool
3. Purée the raspberries with half of the syrup and strain through a fine sieve
4. Purée the apricots with the other half of the syrup and strain through fine sieve
5. Add the lemon juice to both syrups to taste

Note: *The amount of teuille paste made in the previous recipe may seem to be excessive, but this paste can be kept for a considerable time in a cool fridge.*

**All Pebble Mill recipes
from Marian, Danny, Paul and Bob
and gardening expert,
Peter Seabrook
of "Pebble Mill at One"**

SORREL SAUCE (ideal for the fish course)

2 good handfuls of sorrel leaves
1 tbs margarine
¼ cup cream
1 egg yolk
Seasoning

1. Sweat sorrel leaves in margarine
2. Bring cream to JUST UNDER boiling point
   Stir in sorrel
   IT MAY CURDLE — DO NOT PANIC!
3. Take off heat and add egg yolk and stir
   Return to low heat and stir until sauce thickens
   — and UNCURDLES!
4. Season. Turn into a hot bowl or spoon over
   FILLETS OF FISH which are already cooked,

   Serve with boiled new potatoes
   and sweet buttered carrots.

   Finish with apples and cheese —
   or fresh strawberries and cream cheese
             or cream crackers.

Sue Daymond,
Catering Manageress at
Rank Xerox,
London

SUMMERTIME DINNER MENUS

Menu (1)

Seafood Soufflé

Rolled Breast of Chicken

with

Peppered Boursin

A Tossed Salad with Hazelnut Dressing

Parfait of Citrus Fruits

Accompanied by a light sparkling
White Wine (Champagne preferred)
throughout

or

Menu (2)

A Mousse of Watercress

Minute Steaks with Shallots and

Fresh Herbs

Iceberg Lettuce with

Tomato Petals

Meringue Wafers with

Praline Ice Cream

and a

Chilled Mocha Sauce

Accompanied by a Kir Royale as an aperitif
and a
Vieux Chateau Certan (Pommerol)
with the Steak
(no less than 1 bottle per person!!)

241

DESCRIPTIONS *(rather than recipes)*
of the dishes

Menu (1)

The Seafood Soufflé

Individual 2½" soufflé dishes are filled to ½" with small pieces of scallops, lobster tail and poached scampi in a rich lobster sauce. A plain soufflé mixture based on a white fish sauce is placed on top and baked for 10—12 minutes. Served in a lily-folded napkin on plain white liners.

Breast of Chicken with Boursin

The chicken breasts are de-boned and flattened out like escalopes. Spread with peppered Boursin cheese, rolled and tied or skewered. Season with salt only and bake in a very hot oven for 15 minutes. Remove, sprinkle with Parmesan cheese and brown under the grill. Meanwhilè, prepare sauce by swilling out the cooking tray with white wine, reducing, and adding cream.

Parfait of Citrus Fruits

Parfait mixture in three flavours — grapefruit, lime and orange layered in moulds and sandwiched with very thin sponge.

Hazelnut Dressing (Anton Masimann's recipe)

4 fl oz Hazelnut oil — ¾ fl oz Sherry vinegar —
¼ oz finely chopped shallot, seasoning.

continued on next page

Menu (2)

Watercress Mousse

A standard mousse recipe using a cream sauce base, gelatine to fortify, cooled, whipped cream and whites of egg added with finely chopped fresh watercress leaves just before setting point. Placed in duriole moulds and turned out to serve. Accompany with Melba toast.

Minute Steak

Completely trim entrecôtes or fillets of all fat and gristle to allow 6 ozs finished weight. Flatten, brush with oil, finely chopped fresh shallot and herbs to taste (a little chopped/crushed garlic as well if you so wish). Allow to stand for some 10 minutes. Seal very quickly in a dry pan or under a very hot grill. Serve immediately.

Tomato Petals

Simply remove skin from whole tomatoes (usual method). Cut in six pieces, remove pips and internal coarse flesh to give succulent petal shaped pieces.

Meringue Wafers with Praline Ice Cream

Make or buy ice cream. Make very thin meringue wafers by piping in roundels with 1/8th" plain tube, about 2¾in across. Pre-cut ice cream to same size about 1" in depth, sandwich between two meringue wafers — refreeze, dust with icing sugar mixed with chocolate powder. Serve on plain white plate surrounded by chilled chocolate sauce with the addition of Tia Maria liqueur. Decorate with 3 or 4 whole roasted hazelnuts.

Bev Puxley
Head of Professional Cookery
Westminster Catering College
London

SPECIAL KENCO LIQUEUR COFFEE

Recipe specially prepared for this book

When serving Kenco fresh coffee after a meal, and particularly on special occasions, the addition of a liqueur adds that little something.

The secret of a good liqueur coffee is to use top quality, freshly made, fresh ground coffee such as Kenco Traditional.

For 4 people:
One pot freshly made KENCO coffee
4 tsp granulated sugar
4 measures of your favourite liqueur
¼ double cream
4 stemmed glasses

1. Place 1 tsp sugar in each glass
2. Add measure of liqueur to each
3. Fill one glass with coffee
4. Gently pour double cream over back of spoon, allowing it to float on the coffee
5. Repeat with other 3 glasses.

A number of different liqueur coffees can be made. The following are the more popular varieties recommended by KENCO.

Irish	:	Irish Whiskey
Calypso	:	Tia Maria
Gaelic	:	Scotch Whisky
Carribean	:	Dark Rum
Coffee Royale	:	Cognac
Russian	:	Vodka
German	:	Kirsch
Prince Charles	:	Drambuie

**Anina Payne,
Harrison Cowley (Kenco),
Birmingham**

BREW

This was always made by the young on wet days in summer. It doesn't keep indefinitely but then in summer they always liked the "treat" of orange squash.

Today children are more used to squashes and cordials — but the home-made variety always taste better.

5 oranges; 2 lemons; 2 oz citric acid; 3 lb sugar; 4 pints boiling water.

Grate the zest of the oranges and lemons then place in a large bowl with the sugar and citric acid.

Pour the boiling water over all the ingredients.

When cool, add the juice of all the fruit. Strain and bottle. Dilute to taste.

Best kept in a fridge.

Marcia Gay,
Chagford

ORANGES & LEMONS and WHOOPEE!

A devastating Party Drink!

1½ litres Merrydown Cider
½ bottle of the best Gin
2 split Dry Gingers
6 oranges
6 lemons

1. Slice oranges and lemons
2. Float on liquid
3. Put a teaspoonsful of sugar on each slice
   Leave overnight

ONE WINEGLASS RAISES THE ROOF!!

Mrs Nellie Slater,
London

THE WINE CELLAR

There is an old French proverb which tells us that "A Meal without Wine is like a Day without Sun", and the truth of this is now dawning on ever increasing numbers of hosts and hostesses. However, for them the sun is often obscured by a cloud of anxiety over the question "What wine should we drink?"

The problem assumes gargantuan proportions when it is feared that social reputations and even prospects of promotion might be finely balanced on the point of a corkscrew!

The unwritten Eleventh Commandment says "Thou shalt not be caught wineless". Translated this means that when guests turn up without warning, instead of making an ignominious dash to the local supermarket or off-licence for a litre of plonk, you calmly survey your custom-built natural-pine wine rack stocked with a couple of dozen bottles (chosen with great care and discernment!) and say casually ... "Do try a glass of the Brauneberger Juffer Sonnenuhr Riesling Auslese 1975, it is quite delicious. We picked up a few bottles last year when we did our little trip up the Mosel".

Important decision that has to be made is the location of your 'cellar'.

Wines are like rich relatives and demand special attention; it is necessary to treat them with care if·you want to get the most out of them! They do not like draughts (so the garage is no good), they behave unpredictably when subjected to extreme changes in temperature (the attic is a disaster area), vibrations make them go to pieces and they have an aversion to bright sunlight. It is something of a relief to discover that an unheated cupboard somewhere in the middle of the house is eminently suitable; here they can rest peacefully in a recumbent posture until required to put in an appearance.

continued on next page

When trying to calculate quantities required for a dinner party it might be useful to know that a 75cl bottle provides six glasses of wine (4 fl ozs) and that, on average, guests consume half a bottle per person. Another point worth remembering is that certain ingredients are notorious for killing wine stone dead; namely, citrus fruits, pineapple, bananas, malt vinegar, chillies, chocolate, eggs and heavy mayonnaise.

The following wines would make a good nucleus for your cellar. I have chosen them for their versatility and ability to match a variety of dishes (in addition to the ones mentioned in parentheses). They are genuine examples of their kind and should provide interesting drinking, conversation and enjoyment. They are not the cheapest wines on the market but they represent quality and value for money and should be easily obtainable at your local Wine Merchant (not your local supermarket); in short they are first class wines in the middle price bracket.

Pre- or Post-Prandial Wines
(for leisurely enjoyment before or after your meal)
Crémant de Bourgogne Sparkling White Burgundy (dry)
Rheingau or Mosel wine; Spatlese or Auslese quality (elegant, natural sweetness)

Dry, Crisp White Wines
(Pork, Poulty, Shellfish, Salads)
Sauvignon de St. Bris (Yonne, near Chablis)
Californian Fumé Blanc

Medium, Fruity White Wines
(Fish, Poultry, Pâtés, Hors d'Oeuvre)
German Rheinphalz (Estate Bottled); Kabinett quality
Alsace Gewurztraminer (also recommended with highly spiced food)

continued on next page

Full-bodied White Wines
(Veal, Baked Ham, dishes in Cream Sauces, Salmon/ Halibut, etc)
Californian Chardonnay
Chateauneuf-du-Pape (Rhône)

Sweet White Wines
(Desserts, Puddings, Fruit)
Muscat de Beaumes de Venise (S. Rhône)
Monbazillac (Bergerac, Dordogne)

Rosé de Marsannay (Burgundy)
(Lamb, Hors d'Oeuvre, Fish, Cold Meats, Sausages)

Light Red Wines
(Hors d'Oeuvre, Charcuterie, Salads, Terrines)
Beaujolais Crus (eg Fleurie, Brouilly)
Valpolicella (Italy)

Medium Red Wines
(Lamb, Duck, Pork, Veal, Soft Cheeses)
Coteaux d'Aix en Provence
South African Cabernet Sauvignon

Full-bodied Red Wines
(Beef, Game, Goose, Blue and Hard English Cheeses)
Rioja Tinto Reserva (N.E. Spain)
Californian Zinfandel

Claudia Harris M.S.
Moorwood Cottage Restaurant,
Lustleigh, Devon

Claudia is the first woman in the world to become a Master Sommelier.

CATERING for PARTIES

per head

Cocktails:
4—5 savouries 3—4 drinks
Weddings:
4—6 savouries 3—4 drinks; 1—2 sweet foods
Tea Party:
3—4 savouries 2 small cakes; 2 cups tea

(Quantities per bottle)

Sherry Party:	8—10 glasses in a bottle
Wine:	6—8 glasses in a bottle
Champagne:	6—8 glasses in a bottle
Gin or Whisky:	32 cocktails; 20 with soda
Cordials:	20—25 glasses (Add 7 pints water)
Sandwiches:	1 x 1¾ lb loaf; 20—25 slices
	Allow 6 oz butter
Bouchées:	1 lb flaky pastry makes 50
	Allow 1 pint thick sauce
	6—10 oz filling
Cheese Straws:	½ lb pastry makes 100 straws
Cold Meat:	6—7 lb = 25 portions
Potato Salad:	3 lb potatoes; ¼—½ pint of mayonnaise = 25 portions
Rice or Pasta:	2 lb = 25 portions
	1½ oz (uncooked) per portion
Fruit Salad:	6—6½ lb fruit ⎫
	3—4 pints sugar syrup ⎬ 25 portions
	1½ pints cream ⎭
Tea:	2 oz tea: 1 gallon water ⎱ 25—30 cups
	2 pints milk: 1 lb sugar ⎰
Coffee:	8—10 oz ground coffee: 6 pts water
	3 pts milk: 1 lb sugar = 25 teacups
	2—3 oz instant: 6 pts water ⎱ = 25 teacups
	2 pints milk: 1 lb sugar ⎰ = 50 coffee cups

. . . and now for the

washing up . . .

"LIGHT

is the task

when many share

the toil."

from the ILIAD

Hampering or What to take on a Picnic

ASCOT PICNIC

Smoked salmon sandwiches
with Scotch salmon,
brown bread & lemon

or

Charcuterie variée
with French bread & butter
followed by 3 choices
Poached salmon trout
with mayonnaise

or

Crab claws with
mayonnaise

or

Chicken à l'Estragon

All with green salad and potato salad
with spring onions and
vinaigrette

Raspberries or Strawberries and Cream

Duff & Trotter
Palfrey Place,
London SW8 1AR

FONDUE SAVOYARDE

A dish from both French and Swiss Alps — eaten after a day's climbing.

It is simple but enormously satisfying dish, the smell of which makes your mouth water, as you come down the mountains after a long day.

Until the tourists got hold of it, it was the staple diet of the mountain pastoralists of the Alps. They had the homemade cheese, the wine from the valleys below and the bread.

You *should* have a special Fondue dish, stand and heater, and long forks, but you *can* get by without!

1. Rub the inside of an enamelled or earthenware casserole with garlic
2. Put in a glass of good wine per person
3. Heat gently until it begins to boil
4. Then stir in 200—250 grams of grated Gruyère and Emmenthal/or Cheddar and Edam
5. Stir well to a thick bubbling cream
   Season
6. Prepare some bread by cutting it into small squares
   — French bread preferably.

continued

continued

To eat Fondue you place it in the casserole in the middle of the table over a low heat — fondue stove or camping gaz stove turned very low.

Each person dips a square of bread on the end of a fork into the bubbling cheese.

DO NOT DRINK WATER WITH IT, AS IT TURNS
THE CHEESE TO ROCK IN THE TUM!
Glasses of white wine are called for.
He or she who drops her bread into the cheese last,
pays for drinks all round.
As the cheese level drops, you have to eat quicker and quicker, and by the end there will be a marvellous browned patch of toasted cheese in the bottom of the dish that will be forked out and shared among friends.

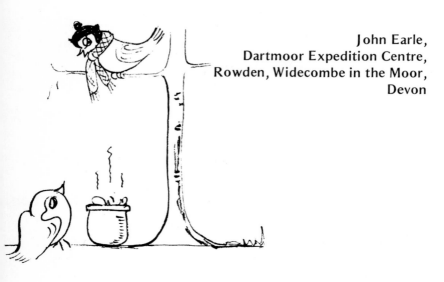

John Earle,
Dartmoor Expedition Centre,
Rowden, Widecombe in the Moor,
Devon

GLYNDEBOURNE PICNIC

First course:

Champignons aux Herbes Fraiches
(Mushrooms in a fresh green marinade of
herbs and white wine)

or

Crab Claws
with home-made lemon mayonnaise

or

Melon and Westphalian Ham

or

Artichokes Vinaigrette
with chopped hard-boiled egg
and parsley
All with French bread and butter

Main course:

Poached Salmon Trout
with sauce verte or
home-made mayonnaise

or

Escalope of Veal
with tomatoes, mushrooms
and spring onions in a
yoghurt sauce

or

Half a Lobster
dressed with cucumber mayonnaise

or

Breast of Chicken
stuffed with cream cheese
bacon and herbs

Duff & Trotter,
Palfrey Place,
London SW8 1AR

OUTDOOR LUNCHEON

A wonderful name for a meal that is not always a great experience.

We have all suffered at some time, I expect, from the "curled-up" sandwiches, the "thermosy" tea, and sand in the cakes.

Let us go back to the Edwardian days and read what *not* to take on a picnic.

"Let us keep away from dull chicken, mayonnaise and such like".

An outdoor luncheon should be as dainty as the pretty lips that may salute it.

1. Take a mould of cold salmon, with the assistance of eggs, a few capers and a suspicion of red pepper. Eat it with the support of cucumber cut into ½" slices, grey-peppered, and touched up with lemon juice
2. *Or* tournedos of beef, delicately grilled, red inside and cold, with tartare sauce
3. *Or* A galantine of veal with a sauce of 1 tbs brown sugar, 1 tbs French mustard, 4 tbs of lemon juice — well mingled
4. For a salad — French beans cooked whole and when cold cut into 1" pieces with a silver knife
5. Follow with an Orange Fool or a Cream Ice made with fresh smashed fruit
6. The best accompaniment is a Moselle Cup:-

    A bottle of 1st rate wine
    Add one of seltzer water
    Insert a sliced, but not peeled
    peach, a sprig of borage
    a wineglass of 1st class brandy
    a wineglass of curaçao
    But no sugar and no cucumber!

7. Finish with coffee and a "Fine Champagne".
    Good appetite be with you!

Jean Nyburg

OUTWARD BOUND FLAPJACK

½ lb margarine
½ lb sugar
¼ lb syrup
1 lb rolled oats
½ tsp salt

1. Take a large saucepan, and melt the first three ingredients, without letting them boil
2. Add oats and salt, mix well, and pack into a greased tin 8" x 12" approx so that the mixture is about 1" thick
3. Bake at 350° F for 25 minutes
   The flapjack should be golden brown
   Leave about ½ hour before cutting into 12 squares and do not remove from tin until lukewarm
   If it does not come out easily, try warming the bottom of the tin slightly.

THIS IS EXCELLENT FOOD TO TAKE
OUT ON THE HILLS
It packs well, and is very nourishing.

Pauline Earle,
Dartmoor Expedition Centre,
Rowden,
Widecombe in the Moor,
Devon

RACING PICNIC

Spare Ribs with Devilled Sauce

A choice of 2 of the following
Sandwiches

Watercress and Cream Cheese

Egg mayonnaise

Ham and mustard

Cucumber and mint

Cumberland Sausages with
a Spicy Dip

Half a small Baguette
filled with Chicken,
Mayonnaise and Lettuce

Raspberries or Strawberries
and Cream

**Duff & Trotter,
Palfrey Place,
London SW8 1AR**